Your Future Paychecks And Raises

(Get Dividend Checks In Your Mailbox Paid To The Order of You!)

Cash Your First Check In 30 To 90 Days

By John Roberts

http://www.LiveLearnAndProsper.com/n

YOUR FUTURE PAYCHECKS AND RAISES - Get Dividend Checks In Your Mailbox Paid To The Order of You!

Copyright © 2017 by John Roberts. All rights reserved.

Published by Live Learn and Prosper, Orlando, Florida. Visit us on the web at http://www.LiveLearnAndProsper.com.

1st edition – Release 24dv14 – 7/5/17. **ISBN:** 9781521849910

CONTENTS

CONTENTS

CONTENTS

1

INTRODUCTION

Figure 1-1. Computer Room
Image courtesy of www.Wikipedia.org

As I walked out of the bank's computer room, blinking into the bright afternoon sunlight, my head was still spinning with the financial secret I had just learned.

I had seen how someone could receive big income and never have to work again.

My stunning revelation had begun early that Saturday morning, many years ago, in Springfield, Missouri. As a young computer programmer at Union National Bank, I was working weekend overtime to test my computer program. It printed quarterly dividend checks for stockholders of the bank.

I was surrounded by all of the massive hardware, printers and large mainframe computer with rows of blinking lights and control switches. And I stared in disbelief at the $5335 check my program had printed ($32,000 in today's dollars).

I couldn't believe the size of the check, and felt sure I must have a program bug. I flipped through the pile of checks my program had printed to mail to the bank's stockholders. Most were for $40, or $70, small amounts that I expected. And here and there, a check for $500, or even a $1000. But the $5335 check had set me on my heels.

It had to be a mistake, I thought. So I grabbed my program listing and looked through my computer code for about an hour. Finally, shaking my head in pure wonderment, I concluded my computer program looked fine, and the check it had printed was correct.

Then slowly, another thought began to creep into my consciousness. Wow, I thought, this person never has to work. They don't have to work overtime on Saturdays like me. They never have to work at all. Because they get these big dividend checks every three months, forever. These checks are just like paychecks to them. So they are making $21,340 a year ($128,000 in today's dollars).

And not working for them.

And that was my first, and rather jolting experience with the power of dividend checks. That if people accumulated enough stocks that paid dividends, they would never have to work again.

But looking back on that fateful Saturday, I know today that I still didn't fully appreciate the situation. What I didn't realize back then was that it got even better.

And that was because many dividend stocks INCREASED their dividend every year. So their checks kept getting bigger. Which was like getting an annual pay raise. In other words, owning good dividend stocks was how you could get paychecks and raises - forever.

So you can understand my dazed mental condition as I left the bank that afternoon many years ago. And those thoughts have stuck with me to this day. Because this story really happened. And it is what this book is all about.

That is to say, how to begin building your paychecks and raises for the future - so you never have to work again. Or at least enough to supplement your income. That is the wonderful opportunity that dividend stocks open up to you.

Now, we won't be starting off with $5335 dividend checks. After all, the stockholder in our story had many shares they'd accumulated over the years. Instead, we'll start with much more modest amounts like $50 per quarter, because this is easily attainable. And we'll show you how you can build it up from there.

But doesn't this idea of building your future paychecks and raises seem interesting? Does that story make you feel excited? And aren't you just a little bit encouraged that an ordinary person can invest in dividend stocks like this, and start building their financial future one dividend stock at a time?

If you answered yes to any of those questions, then this book just might be the solution you've been looking for.

Because it will show you **just what you need to know, to start investing in these dividend stocks.** And we will describe this for you in simple terms you already know, and with companies you are already familiar with.

No complicated theory here. No mind-numbing blitz of technical buzzwords. And we'll use stocks whose products you use every day. Like Apple, Microsoft, Clorox, AT&T and more. And some you use but don't even know it - like Sysco, for example (you probably eat their food, because they supply restaurants and grocery stores).

And we'll describe the few specific steps you can take to get started. So that by the end of this book, you will be able to buy your first dividend stock.

And you won't have to wait around for long to see results either. Because you can get your first dividend check in 30 to 90 days.

And be on your way to building *your future paychecks and raises.*

How To Use This Book

As you read through this book, you'll see how simple it is to start building your future paychecks and raises. And why great companies are eager to send you these dividend checks. You will begin to realize this may be the best way for you to succeed. And how you are just a few steps away from getting your first check. So with that in mind, here's what you'll learn about this exciting approach to stock investing.

Chapter 1, what you are reading now, introduces the idea of Passive Income, money you keep getting but don't have to work for. In my true story you just read, the dividend checks my computer program produced were passive income to those bank stockholders that got them. They didn't have to work for them. The checks just showed up in their mailbox.

To put this in perspective, there are only a few ways in life that you can get passive income. And investing in dividend paying stocks is one of them. And the easiest one too. So that's what you'll learn in this book and what it's all about. How to use dividend stocks to build passive income for yourself.

Then in Chapter 2 we answer the important question, "What Is Dividend Stock Investing?" I think you're going to like this new mindset of getting checks from companies you invest in. It's a different way of thinking about investing. But it's not hard to understand. Just like getting paychecks is not hard to understand.

Interestingly, it's an old concept that has been around for hundreds of years. Yet it's been all but forgotten in our new, internet, dot.com era. Mainly because of all the flashy stories about instant billionaires and big stock increases from small company startups. Like the past startups of Facebook, Google, Amazon and others that have dominated the news.

Now, there's nothing flashy about this way to invest. But which would you rather have - a real check in your mailbox, or a flashy long-shot investment that probably won't pay off?

Then in Chapter 3 we get into "Why Invest In Dividend Stocks?" Getting checks in your mailbox is one great reason, of course. And seeing results quickly is another. But you'll learn many more reasons as well. Some you may not have thought of.

For example, did you know that dividend paying stocks hold the company CEO to a very high performance standard, to make money for you? And for those still hurting from the crash of 2009, that dividend stocks typically perform better than those flashy, speculative stocks when the market is down. True, they can lose money too, but often are less affected by down markets.

And you'll learn many more good reasons to invest in dividend stocks as well.

Next, in Chapter 4, you'll learn about "Key Dates For Your Big Payday." After all, you want to know when you'll get paid. And how often, too. And the good news is that some stocks even pay you monthly. Now that's starting to feel like a paycheck, isn't it? That is, a paycheck that you don't have to work for.

Then in Chapter 5 you'll learn "How To Find Good Stocks To Buy." Like how to tell if a stock is a dividend stock. And if it's a good one. Because some dividend stocks are better than others. But there are some simple clues you'll learn to look for.

And here's the good news. You don't need to do all kinds of complicated analysis. And if you don't even want to bother with the simple clues, you don't need to do that either. Because there are many good places to get dividend stock recommendations. Some are free, and some very modestly priced newsletters that will do the research for you.

I even tell you the names of a couple of newsletters I subscribe to, and you can too. Think about that. As a former New York Stock Exchange licensed stockbroker, I know how to do my own analysis. And I still subscribe. They're that good. And they give you plenty of dividend stocks to choose from.

Next, in Chapter 6, you learn "What You Need To Get Started." And you really only need one thing to get started. And that's a stock market account. Just like you need a checking account to hold your money and do your banking, you need a stock market account to hold your stocks and do your investing.

And we'll tell you how you can open a stock market account. Hint: You can open your stock market account with a single phone call to a broker. And they'll be happy to help you set it up. And I'll even tell you which online broker I have used successfully for years.

Once you've done this, you're one click away from getting started. And here's the other good news. You only need to do this once. Then you're good to go.

Chapter 7 is called "Smart Ways To Buy Dividend Stocks." Okay, once you have a stock account, you'll want to invest in your dividend-paying stocks. Nothing complicated here, since they're as easy to buy as any other stock.

So we'll start by walking you through how to buy your first stock. And with your new online account you can do this in seconds, with the click of a mouse.

And like magic, someone, somewhere in the world, will sell you that stock. And we'll even show you one way you can buy even more of them without a commission, and set the whole thing up on automatic pilot to grow your stock value even more.

Chapter 8 is called "Protecting Your Dividend Stock Investments." This is mainly about WHEN to sell. And it is the hardest question in investing. Not knowing when to sell causes people to take big losses in the stock market. Perhaps you have experienced this as well.

But do you know that there is a simple technique that will keep you from having big losses? Maybe even make a profit when the stock is going down? If you do this, you will be way ahead of most investors. Like the investors and employees at ENRON. Had they used this one technique, and another one we show you as well, they would not have suffered catastrophic losses where most of them got completely wiped out!

But you can protect against this. And we'll show you how.

Then we wrap up in Chapter 9 with "Additional Resources," useful to you as a new dividend stock investor. We cover a number of helpful resources in the book. So this section lists them all for you as a handy reference. And some additional resources are listed as well.

Finally, writing this book has been most gratifying, because I know that many of you can make money with dividend stock investing. And that you'll be encouraged as well, because you'll see results quickly.

So I'm excited for you… as you begin building your **"Future Paychecks And Raises."**

So Who Am I And Why Should You Listen To Me?

So who am I and how can I help you with dividend stock investing?

Well, the short answer is I'm a former financial consultant and New York Stock Exchange Series 7 licensed stockbroker. And I've held many more licenses as well, such as the Series 66 (to operate in all 50 states), Life Insurance, Health Insurance and Variable Annuities.

I worked for one of the large broker dealers in the US, out of my office in Coral Gables, Florida. What that means to you is that for part of my long and varied career, I invested other people's money for them professionally. And I took that responsibility quite seriously.

Also important, on a personal investing note, is that I've been actively investing for over 20 years. I've invested in commodity options - like oil, pork bellies, corn, wheat, gold, etc., stock options, speculative stocks and dividend stocks, to name a few. And I still take the occasional speculative stock flyer.

But through the years, I've become convinced that dividend stock investing is the best way for most stock investors to make money over time. So convinced, actually, that most of my stock investments today are in dividend paying stocks. So you might say I eat my own cooking - that I practice what I preach. I believe in this concept so much I risk my own personal money with it.

Like everyone, even Warren Buffett, I started out knowing nothing about investing. As a young man, I often wondered how some people grow so much wealth. I recall sitting down one night, years ago, in my one bedroom apartment, with pencil and paper, manually calculating interest on my meager savings account. I wanted to see how long it would take to build it up into wealth.

And the answer was that I simply couldn't do it that way. I was disappointed, and puzzled. How did successful people do this?

Slowly, the answer came to me. And it was that stock investing was a big part of the answer. So I began investing in stocks. But my first investments didn't turn out so great - they often lost money. But I kept at it. And through research, trial and error, and tenacity, eventually began to succeed with dividend stocks.

Does my early story, my first investments that didn't turn out so great, have a familiar sound to you? I was, perhaps, an investor just like you. And if I can do it, starting from that humble beginning, and making so many mistakes, I know you can too.

So let's look at how dividend stock investing can increase your wealth. How it can start providing you with paychecks -- and raises.

Let's get to the basic questions. And those are, what is dividend stock investing? And why is it so different?

2

WHAT IS DIVIDEND STOCK INVESTING?

Imagine walking out to your mailbox one day and noticing you have an unusual amount of mail. And a big smile spreads across your face because you know what that means. It means today is your big payday.

With excitement, you head back into the house. And you quickly set aside the normal junk mail, advertising circulars and the bills. You go straight to the stack of official looking envelopes you have left, all return addressed from companies you recognize; companies you own stock in.

Opening the first of these, you take out a check for $201.24 from AT&T. And it says those magic words you love - Pay to the order of YOU!

You open anther envelope from a company called Sysco - they supply food to restaurants and grocery stores. Ahhh, so here's another check for $155.78, again, paid to the order of you. The check reassures you that people are still eating food these days, which you correctly assumed was a very safe bet when you invested.

Then another envelope, this one from Hershey. It seems that people still like chocolate as well, so the chocolate business remains profitable. Your proof of this is another check made out to you for $325.27, that falls out of the envelope onto the floor.

And so you continue to open more envelopes with similar results. That is, checks falling out of them, all paid to the order of you.

When you're done, you open your desk drawer and pull out an envelope pre-addressed to your bank, and reach for a stack of deposit slips. It's going to take you a while to write up all of these deposits to mail in to your bank.

But you don't mind. This is a true labor of love. You are depositing over $1100 dollars of free money that magically appeared in your mailbox today. And you didn't even have to work for it. All you had to do was own stock in these companies, and they gladly sent you these dividend checks.

As you finally lick the deposit envelope, full of checks and deposit slips, you don't even notice the funny taste of the glue on your tongue. Because you're focused on taking this rather thick envelope back out to your mailbox to mail to your bank. It will fatten your bank account in a few days when they process all of your deposits.

And as you raise the red flag on the box, to let the mailman know you have mail to be picked up, the smile you have on your face goes from ear to ear. So big that if your neighbors saw you right now, they would wonder what you are up to.

If only they knew your secret. If only they knew this was why you started investing in dividend stocks a few years ago. Because of the money. Paid to the order of you!

This scene I just described is why dividend stock investing is so different from other stock investing. And it can happen to you too, if you start this investing style. Do you see how it's different than investing in typical, speculative stocks, where you're just hoping the stock value goes up? It's different because the speculative stocks don't send you checks. But dividend stocks do.

Doesn't this seem like a good way to invest? And a way that starts paying off quickly? Anything this good is worth exploring a bit further. So just what is a dividend? And why would a company send you a dividend check?

What Is A Dividend?

Simply put, a dividend is money a company pays to you if you own their stock. Because by owning their stock, you have become one of their business owners. You own part of the business. And so, you own part of the business's profits as well.

Really.

If you own stock in the communications giant AT&T, you are an owner of the AT&T company. If you own stock in Coach Handbags, you are an owner of the Coach Company. And if you own stock in Microsoft, or their competitor Apple, or both, you are an owner of these magnificent, cash-gushing companies.

Now, you are not the complete owner of these companies. You just own a small part of them. And many other people own small parts of them as well. But you are all owners, and so the profits of these companies are divided up and sent to the owners.

That's actually where the word dividend comes from - divided. The company's profits are **divided**, and sent to the owners. And you are one of those owners. So you get you part of the **divided up** profits. You get your **dividend**. You get your profit money. You get your dividend check.

So that's what a dividend is. Money sent to you on a regular basis by a company you own. Pretty simple, yes? And pretty nice too, don't you think.

So let's explore that a bit more. Why do some companies pay dividends, and some don't.

Why Companies Pay Dividends-Your Paychecks

Let's say that you own shares of Hershey stock. And for the next three months, Hershey keeps making chocolate bars and selling them. At the end of three months, they figure out how much money they made selling chocolate bars.

They do this by taking the total amount of their sales, and then subtracting all of their expenses. The money left over is their profit for the past three months (the last quarter).

Now, Hershey can do a number of things with this profit money.

1. They can do nothing with it. They can just keep the cash and put it in the bank in their cash account.
2. Or they can pay off some debt.
3. Or they can invest it back in the business. For example, they could spend some of it creating a new chocolate bar, which might make their sales and profits even bigger in the future.
4. Or they can buy back some of their stock.
5. Or they can divide the profits up and send them to stockholders like you as dividend checks.

So how do these choices affect you?

Option 1 seems like it does nothing for you, but in fact, it does make your investment a little safer. With a bigger bank account balance, the company has more money for any emergencies that might come up.

However, if they already have a big enough cash balance, that's not a very efficient use of profits. And there probably aren't that many emergencies that come up in the chocolate bar business.

Option 2, paying off some debt, would also probably make your investment a little safer. Or as the famous investor Peter Lynch said, "Companies that have no debt can't go bankrupt."

In option 3, investing in developing a new chocolate bar, could increase profits in the future. So that might be a good choice, since your future dividend checks could go up - although you probably wouldn't see any benefit right away.

However, in option 4, buying back some of their stock, might have a quick benefit to you. Because the value of your shares in the company could go up as soon as when they announced the buyback. Or right after they bought back the shares.

That's because if the company bought back some of the stock, there is less stock available in the stock market. And usually, when there is less of something, the price goes up. So your shares would become more valuable.

Finally, in option 5, the company could just divide up the profits and send everyone a dividend check. They may decide they already have enough cash in the bank. And that their debt level is acceptable. And they don't need any more products at the moment. And they don't want to buy back stock right now because the price is high - they only want to buy when the price is low (you know, that buy low, sell high thing).

So since they have no other productive uses for the cash profits, they just decide to send it to the owners - like you. Besides, they know the owners like their stock, and probably invested in it, because it pays dividends. So by constantly sending out dividends, they know people will keep investing in their stock. Which will keep the stock price up.

So it's a win-win situation.

Now in the real world, the company may do any number of the things we listed. They may deposit some of the cash. And start working on a new super duper 5 pound Hershey bar. And pay down some debt. And buy back some stock. And also send out a dividend.

But of all those options, if it is a good dividend paying company like Hershey, **they will be very motivated to at least send out a dividend check.** Good companies that pay dividends take great pride in consistently sending them out, quarter after quarter, year after year.

It's a reputation thing. And it shows the owners, stockholders like you and me, that the company is well managed and profitable.

So that's why companies pay dividends. And that's why we buy their stocks. Because they pay us, the owners, our part of the profits - the dividends.

Why Companies Raise Dividends-Your Raises

Another benefit of good dividend paying stocks is that they keep increasing the amount of their dividend. So not only are you getting your dividend checks over and over (your paychecks), but they grow bigger as well (your raises).

What this means to you is bigger and bigger checks. And over time, they can become quite large.

You might be wondering why companies would increase their dividend. And the answer is much the same as why they pay dividends in the first place.

The companies work hard to grow their business and their profits. They do this by introducing new products, or improving their existing products, selling more of their products, capturing more or the market share from their competitors, and reducing their expenses, to name a few ways.

So all of these activities help them produce more profit every year. And they have the same choices of what to do with their increasing profits as we discussed before. One of those choices is to distribute the extra profit to the stockholders (that's you) by increasing their dividend.

In fact, many companies strive for a reputation of consistently raising their dividend every year. This shows stockholders, and future stockholders, that they have a great deal of confidence in their future.

And this attracts more stockholders to buy their stock. So their stock price will tend to grow. And tend to drop less in a stock market downturn than other stocks. Because people will want to hang on to their dividend stocks. So they will keep getting the increasing dividends.

So now you've seen why companies pay dividends, and often keep raising those dividends. And those are two great reasons to buy dividend stocks.

But it's different than the way most people approach stock investing. So let's explore these two approaches and points of view.

Back To The Future - A New Investing Point Of View

Whenever I mention I was a financial consultant and licensed stockbroker, people always ask me the same question. And they never ask me another question that I think they should ask me.

Can you guess what these two questions are?

Here's the question I am NEVER ASKED. No one ever asks me, "Which stocks pay good dividends?"

The question I am ALWAYS ASKED is, "Which stocks do I think will go up a lot." Or they'll mention stocks they own, and want to know if I think the price will go up. Or they'll mention their 401k stock in the company they work for, which they religiously watch daily, again, wanting to know if I think the price will go up.

This is known as speculation - buying something for a low price and hoping it goes up so you can sell it for a profit. And there's nothing particularly wrong with that.

But in the past, for most of the history of the stock market, that is not the first question that investors used to ask. Their first question was, "How much will the stock pay me?" Because people bought stocks mainly for their reliable and sizeable dividends. The stock price going up was just thought of as a bonus.

See the difference? They weren't speculating. They wanted to know how much their dividend checks would be. And what annual dividend yield percent the stock would pay. So when they saw that a stock paid a 3% dividend, they knew if they bought $1000 of that stock, they would get $30 of dividend payments per year.

This was similar to when people opened savings accounts in the past. I say "was" because today savings accounts pay virtually nothing. But that fact aside, they wanted to know what interest rate they would be paid. For example, if they opened a savings account with $1000, and the bank paid 3% interest, they would get $30 of interest payments for the year. Of course, good luck finding that interest rate today.

So they looked for solid, profitable companies to invest in for the long term. Companies that could keep on paying them dividend checks, quarter after quarter, year after year. Indeed, these types of dividend paying stocks were so reliable they were called widow and orphan stocks. This alluded to their ability to consistently pay dividends to support widows if their husband's died.

A widow and orphan stock that has been around for a long time is AT&T (Symbol T). I have it in my portfolio today, which supports just how durable and reliable this stock has been.

So they bought for the long term, reliable, income producing aspects of the stocks. They didn't think much about whether the value of the stock would rise. That was secondary.

This way of thinking, and these people, can be called investors, as opposed to speculators.

Then in the latter 20th century, along with the internet, the dot.com boom and other spectacular, crazy increases in stock values, people forgot all about dividends. They focused on how high and how fast the stocks they bought would go up - presumably so they could sell them at the higher value for a big, fast profit.

And with all of the flashy, instant millionaire stories that permeate the news, this is probably how most stock buyers continue to think today. My personal experience seems to bear this out. That all most people want is a hot tip, to buy a new stock for a low price. And then presto, just wait six months, and it takes off to make them an instant millionaire.

Now, there is a time and place for some speculation. But the largest gains and the most profitable thing to do is often to invest in dividend paying stocks. To go back to the old way. To invest in stocks that pay you money every quarter, year after year.

And history backs that up. Over 45% of stock market gains come from dividends alone. John D. Rockefeller certainly thought well of this approach when he said, "Do you know the only thing that gives me pleasure? To see my dividends coming in."

Because as dividend stocks continue to pay, and their businesses grow, their price goes up as well - just like the speculators hope for. So dividend stocks are kind of the best of both worlds. They start paying you cash money soon after you buy them. And, they can go up in value too.

Recently, people have begun awakening to the advantages of dividend stocks again. So your timing in buying this book is excellent. Because now you're reading about this new, back to the future, investor point of view, not the prevailing speculator view.

Or put another way, you can begin to think of cash paying dividend stocks like I do.

I like to think of them as money machines.

Think Of Dividend Stocks As Money Machines

Wouldn't it be nice if you could go down to Walmart and pay $49.95 for a money machine? And you could buy as many of them as you wanted. Maybe every week you bought another one. That's fifty-two money machines in a year.

You just set the little money machines in the closet as you buy them and forget about them. And every three months each one dumps $.50 on the floor. That's a little over four cents a week per machine.

So the first week you'd have 4 cents lying on the floor. The next week you buy another money machine and throw it in the closet. So you have two machines, which throw out 8 cents that week on top of the 4 cents from last week. The next week, three machines, so you'd get 12 cents, on and on for fifty-two weeks. At the end of the first year you'd have over 5,512 pennies just lying all over the floor. What a mess. But that's a $55 mess.

And the next year, you'd expect to see 10,816 pennies lying on the floor - because all 52 of your money machines would be working for you all year. Except you notice the little money machines put out 1,081 extra pennies, because they are starting to put out 10% more pennies every year. So they actually put out 11,987 pennies the second year. So now there are 17,499 pennies on the floor, or about $175.

And the pile just keeps growing. Your money machines just keep pumping out more and more money.

That's how good dividend stocks work - they just keep pumping out more and more money every year. And increasing the amount of money each machine pumps out every year. They act like money machines.

Interestingly, a share of Walmart stock, or Microsoft stock, would cost about the same as our theoretical $49.95 money machine, and put out about the same amount of pennies in our example, more or less.

Good dividend stocks act like money machines.

How This Makes Big Money For You

OK, so funny illustrations with money machines and piles of pennies aside, how does this work for you?

Well, the money machines in our example were dividend paying stocks. And the pennies they spit out were dividends. And since the money machines spit out even more pennies per machine each year, those were dividend increases.

So by buying dividend paying stocks that increase their dividends, even if you spend the dividend checks when you get them, you will be making more and more money, because the dividend checks keep getting bigger every year.

Here's how that works. Let's say you buy a dividend paying stock, and the stock price never changes (most unusual). And you just spend the dividend checks whenever they hit your mailbox.

We'll say you bought 100 shares of Microsoft (MSFT) for $35 a share. It pays a 3% dividend when you buy it, and has been increasing the dividend by 10% a year. And the stock price never changes from $35 a share.

The table below shows the results. Now before you look at it, understand this is a pretty conservative scenario. Actually, Microsoft has been increasing their dividend by 12% a year. And historically, stock values have gone up about 7.5% a year on average, instead of staying the same. And again, you are just spending the dividend checks when they come in, not using them to invest in more stock.

So here's what happens…

MSFT Share Price Stays The Same; No Dividend Reinvestment

Initial Dividend %	3.0	1.03
Dividend Increase %	10.0	1 10
Initial Share Price	$35.00	35.00
Share Price Increase %	0.0	1.00
Reinvest Dividends?	n	<-- Enter Y or N for Yes or No
Shares Bought	100.0	

Year	Nbr of Shares	Share Price	Total Stock Value	Div %	Div Per Share	Yearly Paycheck From Div Paid	Shares Bought w/ Divs	Total Divs Paid	Your Total Value	Total Return To Original Investment
A	B	C	D	E	F	G	H	I	J	K
1	100.0	$35.00	$3,500.00	3.0%	$1.05	$105.00	0.0	$105.00	$3,605.00	103.0%
2	100.0	$35.00	$3,500.00	3.3%	$1.16	$115.50	0.0	$220.50	$3,720.50	106.3%
3	100.0	$35.00	$3,500.00	3.6%	$1.27	$127.05	0.0	$347.55	$3,847.55	109.9%
4	100.0	$35.00	$3,500.00	4.0%	$1.40	$139.76	0.0	$487.31	$3,987.31	113.9%
5	100.0	$35.00	$3,500.00	4.4%	$1.54	$153.73	0.0	$641.04	$4,141.04	118.3%
6	100.0	$35.00	$3,500.00	4.8%	$1.69	$169.10	0.0	$810.14	$4,310.14	123.1%
7	100.0	$35.00	$3,500.00	5.3%	$1.86	$186.01	0.0	$996.15	$4,496.15	128.5%
8	100.0	$35.00	$3,500.00	5.8%	$2.05	$204.62	0.0	$1,200.77	$4,700.77	134.3%
9	100.0	$35.00	$3,500.00	6.4%	$2.25	$225.08	0.0	$1,425.85	$4,925.85	140.7%
10	100.0	$35.00	$3,500.00	7.1%	$2.48	$247.58	0.0	$1,673.43	$5,173.43	147.8%
11	100.0	$35.00	$3,500.00	7.8%	$2.72	$272.34	0.0	$1,945.77	$5,445.77	155.6%
12	100.0	$35.00	$3,500.00	8.6%	$3.00	$299.58	0.0	$2,245.35	$5,745.35	164.2%
13	100.0	$35.00	$3,500.00	9.4%	$3.30	$329.53	0.0	$2,574.88	$6,074.88	173.6%
14	100.0	$35.00	$3,500.00	10.4%	$3.62	$362.49	0.0	$2,937.37	$6,437.37	183.9%
15	100.0	$35.00	$3,500.00	11.4%	$3.99	$398.74	0.0	$3,336.11	$6,836.11	195.3%
16	100.0	$35.00	$3,500.00	12.5%	$4.39	$438.61	0.0	$3,774.72	$7,274.72	207.8%
17	100.0	$35.00	$3,500.00	13.8%	$4.82	$482.47	0.0	$4,257.19	$7,757.19	221.6%
18	100.0	$35.00	$3,500.00	15.2%	$5.31	$530.72	0.0	$4,787.91	$8,287.91	236.8%
19	100.0	$35.00	$3,500.00	16.7%	$5.84	$583.79	0.0	$5,371.70	$8,871.70	253.5%
20	100.0	$35.00	$3,500.00	18.3%	$6.42	$642.17	0.0	$6,013.87	$9,513.87	271.8%

Figure 2-1. Microsoft Share Price Stays The Same; No Dividend Reinvestment

In the first year, Microsoft pays you a 3% dividend, and you get a $105 check in the mail. Your total return on your $3500 investment is 103% (column

NOTE: To keep the illustrations simple, I've just calculated and shown the dividend payments year by year - like Microsoft was paying their dividend annually. Actually, Microsoft, and most dividend stocks, pay quarterly. So the real results would be a little different. But this is pretty close, and easier to visualize than a table of 80 quarterly compounding dividend entries.

K). Your stock is still worth $3500 (D), so you still have 100% of your initial investment, plus you got a 3% dividend (E, G). So that's your 103% Total Return To Original Investment (K).

Then you cash the $105 check, and take someone special to a nice lunch at a restaurant on the beach, or something fun like that. In other words, you don't reinvest the dividends, you just spend them.

Year by year, your dividend checks keep increasing. By year 8, they have almost doubled, to $204.62. Okay, so you can take someone special to a nice dinner.

And by year 15, you have received a total of $3336.11 in yearly dividends. Your $3500 investment has almost totally paid for itself. The dividends have bought the stock for you. And from now on it's just all free money. I like that free money thing, don't you?

Finally, by year 20, your $3500 investment, which you still own, plus dividends of $6013.87, has resulted in $9,513.87 total value to you.

That's not too bad for a $3500 investment. And $6013.87 in free dinners.

Or had you not spent the dividends, and left the money in your account, your balance would be $9,513.87.

But you can do a lot better than that.

Because instead of spending the dividends when you get them, or just leaving them in your account, you can use the dividends to buy even more Microsoft stock each year. Or back to our money machines for a minute, what if you spent those thousands of pennies (dividends) to buy even more money machines (stocks), which produced even more thousands of pennies (dividends), with which you could buy even more money machines (stocks)... on and on.

In other words, you literally use your money machines to buy you even more money machines!

When you do this you start **compounding** your wealth. And compounding is one of the most powerful concepts in investing.

Now compounding starts slow, but grows faster and faster over time. It's such a powerful concept and wealth multiplier that Albert Einstein once said, "Compounding... is the eighth wonder of the world..."

And this action of using the money machines pennies (dividends) to buy even more money machines (stocks) is called **dividend reinvestment**. In other words, when you get a dividend check, you don't spend it. You use it to buy more (reinvest in) that dividend paying stock. And this is where you really get the compounding effect on steroids.

DIVIDEND REINVESTMENT: This idea of using your dividends to buy even more shares of your stock is called "Dividend Reinvestment." It's a simple, and powerful investing technique and can create a dramatic increase in your wealth over time.

So if you are not yet retired, or don't need the checks for everyday expenses just yet, this is a powerful way to grow your wealth much more rapidly.

And get this. With dividend reinvestment, and the resulting wealth compounding, you can make money when the stock price goes up, stays the same and even when the stock price goes down! That's right. You can often make money in all three situations. But if you are a speculator, then you can only make money in one of the three situations - when the stock price goes up.

Now that's a pretty incredible claim. So if you only read one chapter in this book, this is the one to read. Because I'm going to show you how that's possible.

So let's start with the earlier situation where you were just spending your dividends. But instead we change it to reinvesting the dividends and see what a difference that makes. Just like before, we'll say that you bought 100 shares of Microsoft (MSFT) for $35 a share. It pays a 3% dividend when you buy it, and has been increasing the dividend by 10% a year. And the stock price never changes from $35 a share. But this time you are reinvesting your dividends.

Here's how that would look...

MSFT Share Price Stays The Same; With Dividend Reinvestment

Initial Dividend %	3.0	1.03
Dividend Increase %	10.0	1.10
Initial Share Price	$35.00	35.00
Share Price Increase %	0.0	1.00
Reinvest Dividends?	y	<-- Enter Y or N for Yes or No
Shares Bought	100.0	

Year A	Nbr of Shares B	Share Price C	Total Stock Value D	Div % E	Div Per Share F	Yearly Paycheck From Div Paid G	Shares Bought w/ Divs H	Total Divs Paid I	Your Total Value J	Total Return To Original Investment K
1	100.0	$35.00	$3,500.00	3.0%	$1.05	$105.00	3.0	$105.00	$3,605.00	103.0%
2	103.0	$35.00	$3,605.00	3.3%	$1.16	$118.97	3.4	$223.97	$3,723.97	106.4%
3	106.4	$35.00	$3,723.97	3.6%	$1.27	$135.18	3.9	$359.14	$3,859.14	110.3%
4	110.3	$35.00	$3,859.14	4.0%	$1.40	$154.10	4.4	$513.24	$4,013.24	114.7%
5	114.7	$35.00	$4,013.24	4.4%	$1.54	$176.27	5.0	$689.51	$4,189.51	119.7%
6	119.7	$35.00	$4,189.51	4.8%	$1.69	$202.42	5.8	$891.93	$4,391.93	125.5%
7	125.5	$35.00	$4,391.93	5.3%	$1.86	$233.42	6.7	$1,125.35	$4,625.35	132.2%
8	132.2	$35.00	$4,625.35	5.8%	$2.05	$270.40	7.7	$1,395.75	$4,895.75	139.9%
9	139.9	$35.00	$4,895.75	6.4%	$2.25	$314.83	9.0	$1,710.59	$5,210.59	148.9%
10	148.9	$35.00	$5,210.59	7.1%	$2.48	$368.59	10.5	$2,079.18	$5,579.18	159.4%
11	159.4	$35.00	$5,579.18	7.8%	$2.72	$434.13	12.4	$2,513.31	$6,013.31	171.8%
12	171.8	$35.00	$6,013.31	8.6%	$3.00	$514.70	14.7	$3,028.01	$6,528.01	186.5%
13	186.5	$35.00	$6,528.01	9.4%	$3.30	$614.63	17.6	$3,642.64	$7,142.64	204.1%
14	204.1	$35.00	$7,142.64	10.4%	$3.62	$739.75	21.1	$4,382.39	$7,882.39	225.2%
15	225.2	$35.00	$7,882.39	11.4%	$3.99	$898.00	25.7	$5,280.39	$8,780.39	250.9%
16	250.9	$35.00	$8,780.39	12.5%	$4.39	$1,100.34	31.4	$6,380.72	$9,880.72	282.3%
17	282.3	$35.00	$9,880.72	13.8%	$4.82	$1,362.05	38.9	$7,742.77	$11,242.77	321.2%
18	321.2	$35.00	$11,242.77	15.2%	$5.31	$1,704.79	48.7	$9,447.56	$12,947.56	369.9%
19	369.9	$35.00	$12,947.56	16.7%	$5.84	$2,159.62	61.7	$11,607.18	$15,107.18	431.6%
20	431.6	$35.00	$15,107.18	18.3%	$6.42	$2,771.82	79.2	$14,379.00	$17,879.00	510.8%

Figure 2-2. Microsoft Share Price Stays The Same; With Dividend Reinvestment

So in the first year, everything starts out like before. Microsoft pays you a 3% dividend, and you get a $105 check in the mail. Your total return on your $3500 investment is 103% (column K). Your stock is still worth $3500 (D), so you still have 100% of your initial investment, plus you got a 3% dividend (E, G). So that's you 103% Total Return To Original Investment (K).

But then, since you are reinvesting the dividends, you don't cash the $105 check and spend it. Instead, you buy three more shares of Microsoft stock with it (3 @ $35 = $105). So now, starting in year 2, you have 103 shares of stock generating dividends, instead of just the original 100 shares like in our earlier example.

Year by year, your dividend checks keep increasing, and you keep reinvesting them into more shares. Because of this, your dividend has grown and doubled two years sooner, by year 6 instead of year 8.

And by year 15, you have received a total of $5280.39 in yearly dividends vs. $3336.11 before. And it took you two years less for the stock to pay for itself. Before, that took 15 years, but now down to 13 years. The extra share's dividends have bought the stock for you faster. AND, you have many more shares, 186.5 now vs. 100 in the original example.

Finally, by year 20, instead of just 100 shares, you now own 431.6 shares, over four times as many. And all of those shares are giving you an annual $2771.82 dividend, vs. only $642.17 by year 20 in our original example. Your total value of your original $3500 investment, plus all the shares bought with the increased dividends, plus year 20's dividend, is $17,879, vs. $9,513.87 total value in our original example.

And here's an even bigger difference. Since you spent the dividends in the original example, you would only have 100 shares of stock and your portfolio would be worth $3500. But in this example, you own 431.6 shares and your portfolio is worth $17,879.

That's an incredible difference in the two results. And you never put another dollar into the stock to achieve it! You simply reinvested the dividends. You let the money machines buy you more money machines.

And remember, this example assumed the stock price never went up. And that would be most unusual for a stock that kept increasing its dividends 10% a year. Because many investors would want to buy it, which would cause the stock to go up over time.

Heck, after reading what I just wrote, I want to buy it. Oh, never mind, I already own Microsoft. For the dividend increase and other reasons as well. But that aside, you see what I mean. The price actually goes up because others want to buy it too.

So let's see how things would work out if the stock value went up. Again, we'll be conservative and say it goes up 4% a year, although we know, historically the stock market has gone up on average by 7.5% a year.

And like before, we'll say that you bought 100 shares of Microsoft (MSFT) for $35 a share. It pays a 3% dividend when you buy it, and has been increasing the dividend by 10% a year. And you are reinvesting your dividends. But now, we'll say the stock price goes up 4% a year.

So here's what happens…

MSFT Share Price Goes Up; With Dividend Reinvestment

Initial Dividend %	3.0	1.03
Dividend Increase %	10.0	1.10
Initial Share Price	$35.00	35.00
Share Price Increase %	4.0	1.04
Reinvest Dividends?	y	<-- Enter Y or N for Yes or No
Shares Bought	100.0	

Year	Nbr of Shares	Share Price	Total Stock Value	Div %	Div Per Share	Yearly Paycheck From Div Paid	Shares Bought w/ Divs	Total Divs Paid	Your Total Value	Total Return To Original Investment
A	B	C	D	E	F	G	H	I	J	K
1	100.0	$35.00	$3,500.00	3.0%	$1.05	$105.00	3.0	$105.00	$3,605.00	103.0%
2	103.0	$36.40	$3,749.20	3.3%	$1.16	$118.97	3.3	$223.97	$3,868.17	110.5%
3	106.3	$37.86	$4,022.89	3.6%	$1.27	$135.01	3.6	$358.98	$4,157.91	118.8%
4	109.8	$39.37	$4,324.22	4.0%	$1.40	$153.50	3.9	$512.48	$4,477.72	127.9%
5	113.7	$40.95	$4,656.83	4.4%	$1.54	$174.84	4.3	$687.32	$4,831.67	138.0%
6	118.0	$42.58	$5,024.94	4.8%	$1.69	$199.55	4.7	$886.87	$5,224.49	149.3%
7	122.7	$44.29	$5,433.47	5.3%	$1.86	$228.22	5.2	$1,115.09	$5,661.69	161.8%
8	127.8	$46.06	$5,888.16	5.8%	$2.05	$261.59	5.7	$1,376.68	$6,149.74	175.7%
9	133.5	$47.90	$6,395.73	6.4%	$2.25	$300.53	6.3	$1,677.21	$6,696.26	191.3%
10	139.8	$49.82	$6,964.11	7.1%	$2.48	$346.12	6.9	$2,023.32	$7,310.23	208.9%
11	146.7	$51.81	$7,602.64	7.8%	$2.72	$399.65	7.7	$2,422.97	$8,002.29	228.6%
12	154.5	$53.88	$8,322.38	8.6%	$3.00	$462.72	8.6	$2,885.70	$8,785.10	251.0%
13	163.0	$56.04	$9,136.51	9.4%	$3.30	$537.30	9.6	$3,422.99	$9,673.80	276.4%
14	172.6	$58.28	$10,060.75	10.4%	$3.62	$625.78	10.7	$4,048.77	$10,686.54	305.3%
15	183.4	$60.61	$11,114.00	11.4%	$3.99	$731.18	12.1	$4,779.95	$11,845.17	338.4%
16	195.4	$63.03	$12,318.98	12.5%	$4.39	$857.21	13.6	$5,637.16	$13,176.19	376.5%
17	209.0	$65.55	$13,703.24	13.8%	$4.82	$1,008.54	15.4	$6,645.70	$14,711.78	420.3%
18	224.4	$68.18	$15,300.25	15.2%	$5.31	$1,191.05	17.5	$7,836.75	$16,491.30	471.2%
19	241.9	$70.90	$17,150.95	16.7%	$5.84	$1,412.14	19.9	$9,248.89	$18,563.09	530.4%
20	261.8	$73.74	$19,305.61	18.3%	$6.42	$1,681.25	22.8	$10,930.14	$20,988.86	599.6%

Figure 2-3. Microsoft Share Price Goes Up; With Dividend Reinvestment

So in the first year, everything starts out like before. Microsoft pays you a 3% dividend, and you get a $105 check in the mail. Your total return on your $3500 investment is 103% (column K). Your stock is still worth $3500 (D), so you still have 100% of your initial investment, plus you got a 3% dividend (E, G). So that's your 103% Total Return To Original Investment (K).

But then, since you are reinvesting the dividends, you don't cash the $105 check and spend it. Instead, you buy three more shares of Microsoft stock with it (3 @ $35 = $105). So now, starting in year 2, you have 103 shares of stock generating dividends, instead of just the original 100 shares like in our earlier example.

But in year 2, the stock price goes up to $36.40 a share. Which means you only buy 3.3 shares with your dividend reinvestment, vs. 3.4 in our earlier flat price example. And year 3, only 3.6 vs 3.9 shares, because now the price is 37.86 a share.

So you're buying less shares. But the value of your total account is already higher. It's now 4157.91 vs. 3859.14 in the earlier example. In just three year you are already up an additional $300 in total value.

And year by year, your dividend checks keep increasing, and you keep reinvesting them into more shares that are going up in value.

Your dividend checks aren't growing quite as fast, because you are buying less shares, because they are getting more expensive. But that is more than made up for by the faster increase in total value in your account. So that by year 15, you total value is $11,845.17 vs. $8780.39. And by year 20, you own 261.8 shares at $73.74 per share for a total value of $20,986.86, vs. a total value of $17,879.00 in our example where the share price didn't go up.

By the way, you could have just bought 100 shares of a similar non-dividend paying stock. As a speculator, you would be hoping for the value to go up. And if it went from $35.00 per share to $73.74 like Microsoft, your account would be worth $7,374. Not bad. But your Microsoft stock, with dividends and reinvestment is worth $20,986.86. That's three times as much and quite a difference. Such is the power of dividends, reinvestment and compounding.

OK, that's well and good, you say. You see where you make money even if the stock stayed the same. And of course you expected to make money if the stock went up. But what if the stock starts going down every year after you invest.

Well, here's where it gets really interesting. So interesting, in fact, I think you're not going to believe the answer.

The short answer is that you can often still make money in this situation. Believe it or not.

So let's look at this. We'll use all the same assumptions as before. That is, you buy 100 shares at $35 a share. And the dividends increase 10% a year and you reinvest them. But this time, we assume the stock GOES DOWN 4%, year after year.

So here's what happens...

In the first year, everything starts out like before. Microsoft pays you a 3% dividend, and you get a $105 check in the mail. Your total return on your

MSFT Share Price Goes Down; With Dividend Reinvestment

Initial Dividend %	3.0	1.03		
Dividend Increase %	10.0	1.10		
Initial Share Price	$35.00	35.00		
Share Price Increase %	-4.0	0.96		
Reinvest Dividends?	y	<-- Enter Y or N for Yes or No		
Shares Bought	100.0			

Year	Nbr of Shares	Share Price	Total Stock Value	Div %	Div Per Share	Yearly Paycheck From Div Paid	Shares Bought w/ Divs	Total Divs Paid	Your Total Value	Total Return To Original Investment
A	B	C	D	E	F	G	H	I	J	K
1	100.0	$35.00	$3,500.00	3.0%	$1.05	$105.00	3.0	$105.00	$3,605.00	103.0%
2	103.0	$33.60	$3,460.80	3.3%	$1.16	$118.97	3.5	$223.97	$3,579.77	102.3%
3	106.5	$32.26	$3,436.57	3.6%	$1.27	$135.36	4.2	$359.32	$3,571.93	102.1%
4	110.7	$30.97	$3,429.06	4.0%	$1.40	$154.76	5.0	$514.09	$3,583.82	102.4%
5	115.7	$29.73	$3,440.46	4.4%	$1.54	$177.92	6.0	$692.01	$3,618.38	103.4%
6	121.7	$28.54	$3,473.65	4.8%	$1.69	$205.83	7.2	$897.84	$3,679.48	105.1%
7	128.9	$27.40	$3,532.30	5.3%	$1.86	$239.83	8.8	$1,137.67	$3,772.14	107.8%
8	137.7	$26.30	$3,621.25	5.8%	$2.05	$281.73	10.7	$1,419.40	$3,902.98	111.5%
9	148.4	$25.25	$3,746.86	6.4%	$2.25	$334.01	13.2	$1,753.41	$4,080.87	116.6%
10	161.6	$24.24	$3,917.63	7.1%	$2.48	$400.16	16.5	$2,153.57	$4,317.80	123.4%
11	178.1	$23.27	$4,145.09	7.8%	$2.72	$485.14	20.8	$2,638.72	$4,630.23	132.3%
12	199.0	$22.34	$4,445.02	8.6%	$3.00	$596.12	26.7	$3,234.83	$5,041.14	144.0%
13	225.7	$21.44	$4,839.49	9.4%	$3.30	$743.67	34.7	$3,978.50	$5,583.16	159.5%
14	260.3	$20.59	$5,359.83	10.4%	$3.62	$943.74	45.8	$4,922.24	$6,303.57	180.1%
15	306.2	$19.76	$6,051.43	11.4%	$3.99	$1,220.90	61.8	$6,143.13	$7,272.32	207.8%
16	368.0	$18.97	$6,981.43	12.5%	$4.39	$1,613.94	85.1	$7,757.07	$8,595.37	245.6%
17	453.0	$18.21	$8,251.56	13.8%	$4.82	$2,185.75	120.0	$9,942.82	$10,437.31	298.2%
18	573.0	$17.49	$10,019.81	15.2%	$5.31	$3,041.20	173.9	$12,984.03	$13,061.02	373.2%
19	747.0	$16.79	$12,538.58	16.7%	$5.84	$4,360.69	259.8	$17,344.72	$16,899.27	482.8%
20	1006.7	$16.11	$16,223.30	18.3%	$6.42	$6,464.99	401.2	$23,809.71	$22,688.29	648.2%

Figure 2-4. Microsoft Share Price Goes Down; With Dividend Reinvestment

$3500 investment is 103% (column K). Your stock is still worth $3500 (D), so you still have 100% of your initial investment, plus you got a 3% dividend (E, G). So that's you 103% Total Return To Original Investment (K).

But then, since you are reinvesting the dividends, you don't cash the $105 check and spend it. Instead, you buy three more shares of Microsoft stock with it (3 @ $35 = $105). So now, starting in year 2, you have 103 shares of stock generating dividends, instead of just the original 100 shares like in our earlier example.

Year by year, your dividend checks keep increasing, and you keep reinvesting them into more shares. But look at year 2. The stock price dropped from $35 a share to $33.60. So when you reinvest your dividends and buy shares, because of the lower price, you buy 3.5 shares instead of 3.4 shares.

OK, no big deal, right? You only bought a tenth of a share more. And like before, your dividend has grown and doubled two years sooner, by year 6 instead of year 8 in our original "spend your dividends" example. But you can see the dividend has grown a little bit.

And here's the thing. These numbers, your dividends and the number of shares you are buying, are going to start growing faster and faster. Remember we said that compounding starts off slow, and then begins to grow faster and faster, right?

And by year 15, you have received a total of $6,143.13 in yearly dividends, vs. our last example at $4779.95 when the stock price was going up. And by year 20, your total value for your account is $22,688.29 vs. $20,986.86. Wow. You made even more money when the stock was going down than when the stock was going up. And, you now own 1006.7 shares vs. just 261.8 shares when the stock was going up. And those 1006.7 shares are generating $6,464.99 in dividends for the year vs. $1681.25 when the stock was going up.

In other words, just this one stock is giving you over $500 a month in income if you chose to take it. And this happened when the value of the stock, the stock price, was going down!

How is that possible?

And the answer is that since the stock price is going down, you are accumulating more and more shares. And these shares are still paying increasing dividends. So the more shares you own, the bigger the dividend checks. Which means you can buy even more, cheaper priced shares.

And the thing just kind of snowballs once it gets started. It's the old "buy low, sell high" investing maxim on steroids. Except you aren't selling, you are buying lower and lower each time.

Which means when you are doing your original investing, that is, you aren't yet using the dividends for income, it's actually better if the share price doesn't go up much. In this accumulation phase, you want to buy as many shares as possible, as cheaply as possible, so eventually you will get bigger dividend checks when you start relying on them for income.

Now, realistically, you probably won't run into this situation of buying and reinvesting in a stock that keeps going down 4% a year for twenty years. And a stock going down 4% a year for twenty years could indicate problems with the company and the dividends get cut. But it clearly illustrates the point that it is theoretically possible to make money with some dividend stocks even when the price goes down.

Which is quite different from a speculator, who would have lost a lot of money in this situation instead of making money. Our hapless speculator, who invested $3500 in a non-dividend paying stock, would now only have $1611 (100 shares X $16.11 a share), for a loss of over $2000. That's a huge difference compared to our $22,688.29 total value in this last example.

So we've shown in a number of examples where you have a good chance to make money with dividend paying stocks, with dividend reinvestment, if the stock stays the same, goes up or goes down.

But what's real?

What is a realistic scenario and expectation?

Well, let's take Microsoft one more time. And say you bought it at $35 a share. This is real. I did this a few years ago.

And it pays a 3% dividend. But it increases the dividend by 12% - which is real as well. And the stock price goes up on average of 7.5% - which is what the stock market has historically averaged over time.

Now note, there are no guarantees on this investment outcome. But all of the assumptions are based on known historical data. So that said, it would look like Figure 2-5 on the next page.

By year 6, your yearly dividend check would have doubled from $105 to $217.26. By year 15 it would have gone up 8 times to $884.79 and your total value would have gone from $3500 to $17,495.36. And by year 20, your total value would be $33,665.22 with 228.5 shares. And those shares would be generating an annual dividend of $2066.22, or $172 a month.

Just from that one stock - that original $3500 investment. And theoretically, it will just keep paying you more and more per year.

MSFT More Realistic Assumptions; Share Price Goes Up; With Dividend Reinvestment

Initial Dividend %		3.0	1.03							
Dividend Increase %		12.0	1.12							
Initial Share Price		$35.00	35.00							
Share Price Increase %		7.5	1.08							
Reinvest Dividends?		y	<-- Enter Y or N for Yes or No							
Shares Bought		100.0								

Year	Nbr of Shares	Share Price	Total Stock Value	Div %	Div Per Share	Yearly Paycheck From Div Paid	Shares Bought w/ Divs	Total Divs Paid	Your Total Value	Total Return To Original Investment
A	B	C	D	E	F	G	H	I	J	K
1	100.0	$35.00	$3,500.00	3.0%	$1.05	$105.00	3.0	$105.00	$3,605.00	103.0%
2	103.0	$37.63	$3,875.38	3.4%	$1.18	$121.13	3.2	$226.13	$3,996.50	114.2%
3	106.2	$40.45	$4,296.24	3.8%	$1.32	$139.90	3.5	$366.03	$4,436.14	126.7%
4	109.7	$43.48	$4,768.86	4.2%	$1.48	$161.79	3.7	$527.83	$4,930.65	140.9%
5	113.4	$46.74	$5,300.45	4.7%	$1.65	$187.36	4.0	$715.18	$5,487.81	156.8%
6	117.4	$50.25	$5,899.39	5.3%	$1.85	$217.26	4.3	$932.44	$6,116.65	174.8%
7	121.7	$54.02	$6,575.40	5.9%	$2.07	$252.29	4.7	$1,184.73	$6,827.69	195.1%
8	126.4	$58.07	$7,339.77	6.6%	$2.32	$293.41	5.1	$1,478.14	$7,633.17	218.1%
9	131.5	$62.42	$8,205.66	7.4%	$2.60	$341.75	5.5	$1,819.89	$8,547.41	244.2%
10	136.9	$67.10	$9,188.47	8.3%	$2.91	$398.70	5.9	$2,218.60	$9,587.17	273.9%
11	142.9	$72.14	$10,306.21	9.3%	$3.26	$465.92	6.5	$2,684.52	$10,772.14	307.8%
12	149.3	$77.55	$11,580.05	10.4%	$3.65	$545.43	7.0	$3,229.95	$12,125.47	346.4%
13	156.4	$83.36	$13,034.88	11.7%	$4.09	$639.65	7.7	$3,869.60	$13,674.53	390.7%
14	164.0	$89.61	$14,700.12	13.1%	$4.58	$751.56	8.4	$4,621.16	$15,451.69	441.5%
15	172.4	$96.34	$16,610.57	14.7%	$5.13	$884.79	9.2	$5,505.95	$17,495.36	499.9%
16	181.6	$103.56	$18,807.51	16.4%	$5.75	$1,043.75	10.1	$6,549.70	$19,851.26	567.2%
17	191.7	$111.33	$21,340.10	18.4%	$6.44	$1,233.87	11.1	$7,783.57	$22,573.97	645.0%
18	202.8	$119.68	$24,267.02	20.6%	$7.21	$1,461.84	12.2	$9,245.42	$25,728.86	735.1%
19	215.0	$128.65	$27,658.53	23.1%	$8.07	$1,735.89	13.5	$10,981.31	$29,394.42	839.8%
20	228.5	$138.30	$31,599.00	25.8%	$9.04	$2,066.22	14.9	$13,047.52	$33,665.22	961.9%

Figure 2-5. Microsoft More Realistic Assumption; Share Price Goes Up; With Dividend Reinvestment.

3

WHY INVEST IN DIVIDEND STOCKS?

At this point, you understand how dividend stock investing is different. And how you can actually think of these stocks as money machines.

We've seen how that's miles apart from the typical stock speculators mindset. They only have one way to make money on their stocks, and that is if the price goes up.

So let's recap the advantages of dividend stock investing up to this point. And look at the many other advantages as well. Because, as you will see, there are many more we haven't touched on yet.

Quick Results - Your First Check In 90 Days Or Less

One of the biggest advantages to dividend stock investing is that you see quick results. Instead of waiting around, hoping your stock will go up, you see money much sooner. You'll see it when the first dividend check hits your mailbox.

Note that most investors just have the dividend paid into their stock account for convenience. But we'll continue with the check in the mailbox image, as I think it's easier to visualize the advantages of dividend stock investing.

You can get your first check in three months or less after reading this book and buying your first dividend stock. This is because they typically pay every quarter, and some even monthly.

Here's a real example for you. This is something you could do right now (please note the prices will have changed since I wrote this).

Let's say its January 1 when you are reading this. You can buy 100 shares of AT&T stock (Stock Symbol T) for $40 a share, for a total of $4000 invested. If you do this, AT&T will send you a check for $50 around February 1st.

Really. It's that fast and that simple.

HOW'S THIS FOR REAL? As I was writing this chapter on 8/27, I had received a dividend check from AT&T three weeks earlier on 8/1, and will get my next check around 11/1.

Now maybe $50 doesn't sound like much, but consider this. They will send you another $50 check on May 1st - just three months later. And another on August 1st, and another on November 1st - just in time to buy your Thanksgiving turkey with it. So your AT&T stock will pay you $200 a year. That's 5% you are getting on your money.

To put that in perspective, bank savings account rates are a paltry .1% to 1.00%. And here you are getting 5% with AT&T. So you are earning at least 500% or more with AT&T than with a savings account. That's a huge difference.

So you are getting a great return, and quickly. That's a big advantage. And quick results like this will encourage you to continue dividend investing. And that's another benefit as well.

Most Simple - Set It And Forget It

Another great advantage to investing in dividend stocks is how simple it is. For starters, dividend stocks are just as easy to buy as other stocks. And after that, you can pretty much set it and forget it. You just watch the dividend checks roll in every month to three months.

There are only two other times that you will take any further action. One is if the stock value drops too much. And we give you a very simple way to know this later on in the book.

The other time is if the company decides to cut or eliminate its dividend. Since companies are quite motivated to keep paying continuous dividends, this doesn't happen that often, but needs mentioning.

And if you bought the stock on a recommendation from a newsletter, they will typically alert you to either of these events. So outside of those two events, you just hang on to the stocks, keep collecting the dividend checks, and watch them grow.

How simple is that.

NOW HERE'S A LONG TERM INVESTOR: Warren Buffett started buying his Coca-Cola shares in 1987. And now, almost 30 years later, he owns 400,000,000 shares.

And he gets an annual dividend of $1 a share. That's a $400,000,000 check in his mailbox! No wonder he hangs onto the shares. Clearly, Coke is it.

By the way, speaking of management motivated to continuously pay dividends, Coca-Cola has paid and raised its dividend for 53 consecutive years. So next year, Warren's dividend check will almost certainly be bigger still.

You Avoid The Market Timing Dilemma

Now contrast dividend stock simplicity to what you have to do when you are speculating.

Remember that speculating is how most people think about stock investing. That is, you are buying a stock at a low price, to later sell at a high price, to make your big profits.

With dividend stocks you see your profits rolling in every three months with your dividend checks. So you don't do anything. You just watch your dividend checks roll in. Those are real profits and real money going into your account.

But when do you get your profits from speculative stocks? When does that money roll into your account? Sure – your stock may be up, so you show paper profits. But to take your profits, to make them real, you have to sell the stock.

You have to constantly watch the stock value, trying to decide when to sell them at a profit. If you bought a stock at $40 a share and it goes to $60 a share, do you sell now and take the $20 profit? Or do you hang in there, hoping it will go to $70 a share for a $30 profit?

How do you decide? Because now you're trying to guess what the market is going to do (called timing the market). Your profit depends on it. You have to get your timing right. And almost no one can time the market correctly. Because no one knows what the market is going to do.

So let's say you hang in there, hoping for $70 a share, and then your stock starts going down to $55 a share. Hmmm... now you're wishing you had sold at $60. But you think, well, maybe it will come back up to $60, so you hang in there some more. And it goes down to $38. Now you're losing money. You accidently turned a profit into a loss. What do you do now - sell it at a loss? Or hang in there some more?

Believe me, you will agonize over this. And this is the typical experience of a speculator. And they often wind up losing money - after all of that worry.

And no wonder. Knowing when to sell a stock is one of the hardest things to do in investing. Even Warren Buffett says he has trouble with it. Why? For the same reason we said above. He doesn't know what the market is going to do either. No one does.

But with dividend stocks, you don't have all of this agonizing going on. We give you the simple rule to know when to sell the stock. And if that rule doesn't apply, you just hang on and keep collecting the dividends.

See the difference? You just don't worry so much. And in the meantime, you see your profits just keep rolling in.

WHERE ARE THOSE BIG PROFITS? Most people speculate on stocks to make big profits. But according to a recent Forbes article, the average investor only makes somewhere between 1.9% and 2.6% annually, depending on the time frame.

It's quite easy to find dividend stocks that pay 3-4%, and a few as high as 10%. And they increase their dividend. And you don't have to worry about when to take your profits - you see them every three months in your dividend checks. Oh, and the value of these stocks will probably go up as well.

You Get Raises

Another big advantage, which we've already alluded to, is that you get raises. The best dividend stocks raise their dividend.

Compare that feature to other typical investments. It is unlikely that savings accounts, or CD's are going to raise their rates very much in the future, if at all. And when you own bonds, they are for a fixed rate, so no raise is going to happen there.

But when you buy dividend stocks, many of them consistently raise their dividend, year after year.

It's like if a banker started a dream savings account. And he told you, hey, if you put $4000 in this dream savings account, I will pay you 5% interest the first year. Then I will increase the interest rate by a little each year.

Now, it's unlikely you will ever see that kind of dream savings account. But that is how our dividend stocks act. Kind of like the dream savings account I just described. And this is not just some theoretical exercise.

For example, over the past five years, AT&T has raised their dividend by about 4 cents a share every year. So you are getting about a 2% raise to your dividend, your paycheck, every year. That's about like the typical pay increases at work these days.

So if you owned 100 shares of AT&T stock, you would be getting quarterly dividends of about $50 a share, or $200 a year. Then next year, quarterly dividends of $51, or $204 a year. And the next year about $52 per quarter or $208 per year.

It's a good bet you will keep getting these dividends and raises on and on, year after year. And over time this adds up.

Just look at how consistently AT&T has raised their dividend - see chart below.

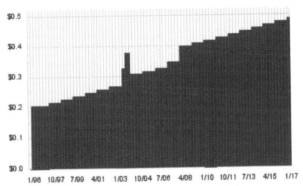

Figure 3-1. AT&T Dividend History Chart
Image courtesy of www.DividendChannel.com

It's a lot like the dream savings account we described. Except it is real. You keep getting dividend checks, and the checks keep getting bigger. In other words, you get raises.

And many dividend stocks have even greater raises. And these can turn into impressive yields over time.

You Get Impressive Yields Over Time

How would you like to earn over 10% on your money? That's an unheard of rate these days. But it's possible with good dividend paying stocks over time.

This is because some dividend stocks raise their dividends by a large amount each year. Much greater than the increases we just looked at for AT&T. Like Microsoft, for example. Microsoft has been increasing their dividend by over 10% a year.

We explored this in an earlier chapter in detail. But it's worth looking at again at a high level, focusing just on the dividend increase.

So let's say you bought 100 shares of Microsoft at $35 a share. And at that time, Microsoft was paying about a 3% dividend (this is called a dividend yield). And Microsoft kept increasing their dividend by 10% year after year.

Then the next year they would pay you 3.3% on your original investment (that's a 10% increase to the original 3% yield). The following year, that would grow to 3.6%. And keep growing until by year ten, you are making an impressive 7.1% on your money, and by year fifteen, a whopping 11.4% yield.

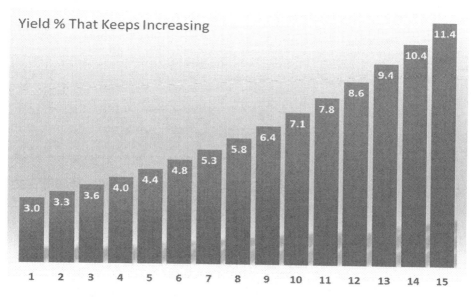

Figure 3-2. A 3% Yield Increasing By 10% Per Year

Now an 11.4% yield might be suspicious if that was what a stock offered immediately (although there are some stocks that can actually do this). There would be questions about if they could keep paying such a large dividend over time.

But it's quite reasonable for many companies when you start out at 3%, and it grows to this amount over time. That's very sustainable when you do it that way.

So you can see this is quite possible. Indeed, it's similar to an investment I made in Microsoft a few years back. And I still own Microsoft. And I'm getting a bigger yield each year, just like our example.

To use a real world example, if you bought Microsoft today, you would pay $63 a share and that would pay you a dividend of $1.56 per share for a yield of 2.5% based on your $63 purchase price. But I bought it at $35 a share a few years ago. And the dividend has increased year by year to the current $1.56 per share – just like you would get if you bought it today.

But my yield is now 4.4%, almost double the current 2.5%, because my cost was $35 per share. And my yield will probably keep going up, year by year as Microsoft keeps raising its actual dividend per share, and I will always be comparing that to my original $35 a share purchase price.

So next year my yield will probably be 4.8% (see chart above), the following year 5.3%, on and on. So over time I will be getting impressive yields. And this will work for you too.

Actually, it's even better than I described because I was conservative with my example. I used a 10% dividend increase just to keep the math easy. But Microsoft has been increasing their dividend by about 12% in recent years, so the yield is actually going up faster.

So, like our banker example earlier, this is like a savings account that keeps increasing the interest they will pay you on your savings. The difference is you won't find a savings account that does that. In fact, interest rates have been going DOWN over the past ten years.

But you can find any number of dividend stocks that will do what Microsoft did - or better.

So not only do you start getting paid as soon as you invest in one of these stocks, you can look forward to getting paid more and more, year after year - barring any unusual circumstances.

This is one of the greatest benefits to you when you invest in dividend paying stocks. They really act like money machines. Indeed, this one aspect can lead to creating real wealth over time.

NOTE: You may already be getting an impressive dividend return and not even know it. If you work for a company with a dividend paying stock, that allows you to buy shares through a 401k or stock purchase plan, this could be happening for you. If you have worked at the company for a long time, you are probably getting an incredible yield on the stocks you bought years ago. That's because the dividend may have kept going up. But your original lower purchase price remains the same.

You might want to check that out with your company stock, if they pay dividends. Just look up the price you paid for the first shares you bought when you enrolled in the plan. Then divide that price into the dollar amount of the current annual dividend.

For example, let's say your company shares were $19.00 a share fifteen years ago when you enrolled in the plan. And today the annual dividend your company pays per share is $1.50. So you are now getting a 7.9% yield on your original shares ($1.50 X 100 / 19.00).

Sweet! You're a dividend stock investing genius and didn't even know it. Now just extend that idea to other dividend paying stocks you can buy.

They Can Be Very Profitable

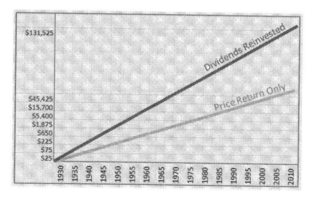

Figure 3-3. S&P 500 Historical Dividend versus Non-Dividend Returns

So typically, how much can these money machines affect your income and wealth? Quite a bit, really. It works out that dividends can contribute close to half of the total investment return of a stock over time.

Specifically, looking at the Standard and Poor's 500 Index (essentially the largest 500 US stocks), the dividends were responsible for 44% of the total return over the last 80 years. And in another study, 40% of the S&P 500's total return came from reinvested dividends between 1935 and 2007.

The chart above shows the return from the stocks in the S&P 500 from 1930 to 2010. It shows two lines. One is with no dividends. The other is with dividends that were reinvested. Reinvesting the dividends greatly increases the returns. The difference is quite striking.

So dividends can clearly be a big part of your investing profit.

The Stock Buys Itself For You Over Time

One of the things I really like about dividend stocks is how the dividend actually helps buy the stock for you.

I'm really big on this concept. For example, I also own rental property. And one of the things I really appreciate with rental property is that the tenants are buying the property for me. Similarly, dividend stocks will help buy themselves for you. The constant dividends you receive are like renters paying for your property.

Here's a real-world example where almost half of the profits I've made from a stock have come from the dividends alone. This squares with our earlier mention where dividends were responsible for 44% of the total S&P 500 stocks return over the last 80 years.

The stock is Calamos Convertible and High Income Fund (CHY). So as I look at it in one of my trading accounts, I see it's just paid a dividend of $59.50. Now $59.50 will not make you wealthy in and of itself. I'm sure we can agree on that. But this stock can clearly illustrate how dividends can create real wealth for you. And this one pays dividends monthly instead of quarterly, so it feels like a free paycheck as well.

Note that I think of Calamos as a "stock-like" investment. Technically it's a closed end fund, not an individual stock like we've used in other examples. That is, it's a fund made up of a mix of convertible securities and high yield bonds. But for our purposes, it trades just like a dividend stock, with a symbol like a stock, which you can buy and sell like a stock, and it pays dividends like a dividend stock. So to keep things simple, I'll just refer to it as a stock.

As you will see, these stock-like investments can be pretty profitable, and I explain them and their profit potential for you in my future book entitled **Make More Money With Special Stock-Like Investments.**

So every month, this Calamos Convertible and High Income Fund (CHY) has deposited $59.50 into my account like clockwork.

I bought 700 shares of CHY in early 2009 during the stock market crash. So I was able to buy at a good price of $8.62 a share for a total investment of $6000 (I'll use round numbers in my examples to keep it easy).

So looking over my statements, I noted that I had collected three and a half years of monthly dividends. That's a total of $2500 I have already collected from this $6000 investment.

My profit is almost half of my original investment - from dividends alone!

And there is no reason to believe I wouldn't keep receiving another $59.50 in my account every month going forward.

So the company has already bought almost half of the stock for me. And it's pretty easy to assume that it will be totally paid for in 8 years. And that's not counting how much faster it will be paid for with dividend increases − I've ignored those just to keep the math easy.

But here's the other good news. The stock is really almost totally paid for already. Because dividend stocks don't just pay dividends. Many of them grow in price as well - like you hope for with speculative stocks.

Dividend Stocks Can Grow Too

So just because you focus on dividend stocks doesn't mean you give up growth in stock value. Remember that I paid $8.62 a share for this CHY stock. But since then, CHY has kept increasing in value to $12.49 a share. So I've made another $2700 on the price increase.

That's growth in stock value. That's money made. That's investment profit.

So while I was collecting all of those dividend checks, month after month, something else happened.

I made a whopping 45% in growth on the stock as well. That price increase from $8.62 a share to $12.49 a share made another $2700 for me.

So in total, I have made $5200 in three and a half years on a $6000 investment. I have almost doubled the investment. It has almost paid for itself completely. And thirteen more months of dividend payments, even assuming no price increase, will bring that total up to the original $6000 investment. That will work out to be $3300 in dividends and $2700 in price appreciation.

I will have doubled my money in four and a half years. The investment will have paid for itself entirely. And all of my investment capital will have been returned to me.

Everything from then on is pure profit.

So you can see how dividend stocks can help buy themselves and grow too. And doubling your money in four and a half years through dividends and stock appreciation is real wealth creation. Because you can scale this up. You can buy more shares than I used in our example.

See why I said early on that dividends can be valuable to your investment success? And build wealth for you. And future income. And all of this started from a measly $59.50 monthly dividend.

By the way, I was actually pretty inefficient with this investment. I didn't even reinvest the dividends in this real-life example. Dividend reinvestment would have really turbocharged that return, like we saw in the earlier Microsoft examples. And we'll talk even more about that later as well.

But the key takeaway from this chapter is that dividend stocks can grow too. So the lesson learned here is that you will probably get some growth on your dividend paying stocks. It's just that we focus on the dividend checks and raises. The growth is just gravy.

But that's some good gravy.

It's Like Buying Stocks At A Discount

Here's another way to think of dividend stocks. It's like buying stocks at a discount.

Everyone likes to buy things at a discount, and I'm sure you feel the same way. For example, there are any number of charge cards these days that give you a 1% or 2% rebate on your purchases. That's really just giving you a one-time discount on those purchases. I have a number of these cards, and you probably do too.

Similarly, you can think of a stock's dividend as a discount, or rebate on your purchase price.

For example, let's say you buy $1000 of stock in a company that pays a 3% dividend. Then after one year of collecting the dividends, you effectively bought those shares at a 3% discounts. You have collected $30 in dividends. So you really paid just $970 for that $1000 worth of stock.

And some stocks pay even more than a 3% dividend, in which case your discount is even greater.

And this is not just a one-time discount. You keep getting this discount to your purchase price over and over again, with each new dividend check. If you hold that stock long enough, at some point all of your dividends (think discounts in this case) will eventually add up to 100%. In other words, it's free. The stock will have bought itself for you like we mentioned earlier.

And... you have more dividend payments that will come in after that!

Now that's some kind of discount, don't you agree?

They Are More Stable During Bad Economic Times

At this point you might be thinking, well this sounds too good to be true. So these stocks are probably more risky than stocks that don't pay a dividend. After all, we've all heard that higher rewards equal higher risks.

But often, just the opposite is true. When the economy or stock market goes down, the dividend paying stocks tend to not go down as much as the stocks that don't pay dividends.

That's because these are the last stocks people want to sell. They want to hang on to their dividend paying stocks if possible. Why? So they can keep getting the dividend checks. And keep getting the dividend increases. And keep their yield percent going up, year over year.

Here's a great example of that. During the Brexit, when Britain voted to leave the European Union, the British pound went down 8% overnight, and the foreign stock markets fell by 8% or more. Even the US stock market was effected, as the Dow went down 610 points to 17400. That was 3.4% in one day. And many big stocks took a 5% haircut.

That's pretty alarming.

But Clorox, that little old dividend-paying bleach company Clorox, WENT UP 1%, amidst all of the turmoil. So not only did the stock lose less than other stocks, it actually gained.

Why? Probably because most people that owned it wanted to keep it for the dividend, and others wanted to buy it to get the dividend. Because Clorox has a long history of being stable, consistently paying a dividend, and increasing that dividend.

And stability looked really good at that time.

So even though the world seemed to be coming apart, investors knew that people were still going to keep washing and bleaching their clothes. And everyone recognized the name Clorox. Because they probably used Clorox, and their Mothers and Grandmothers before them. And you and I probably do too… actually, I do use Clorox, and come to think of it, I have all of my life.

So it was a real safe bet that people would keep using Clorox products for years to come. So suddenly, with the world coming apart, many people wanted to own dividend paying Clorox stock. And the price increase reflected that.

Now that's stability for you.

So you see, with dividend-paying stocks, you get the benefit of being paid while you invest in them (your paychecks), and they are often more reliable and stable as well.

More reliable and stable sounds good in the context of future paychecks.

What's not to like about that?

You Can Buy Some Fat Paychecks In A Down Market

Of course, dividend stocks are not totally immune from market downturns. They can go down in price too. But usually, their price won't drop as much as non-dividend paying stocks. But when they do go down, they often provide a great buying opportunity. Because when the price of the stock goes down, their yield goes higher. Meaning you can buy some fat paychecks at bargain prices.

For example, let's take an exaggerated case with a stock that costs $50 a share and pays a 3% dividend. If the stock drops to $25 a share, then its dividend is now 6%. In other words, the stock price was cut in half, so if the dividend remains the same, then the yield doubles. You are getting twice as much money on your purchase price. You can buy twice as much paycheck for your money.

This is where smart dividend stock buyers jump in and buy at the new low price. Now they have a stock that is yielding 6%.

And even though the stock price will probably start going up, they are still getting that 6% yield. Because the yield to YOU is based off of what YOU paid for the stock, not what it is currently priced at in the stock market.

Note that I am being kind of loose with the terms yield, return, etc., just to keep things simple. In all cases I am simply talking about how much money you are getting in dividends compared to the cost of the stock to you. That is, how much money are you making on your investment as a percent.

We'll leave the precise definitions to the financial geeks.

Jim Cramer, television personality and former hedge fund manager, actually has a name for this situation. He calls these stocks accidental high yielders. Because, due to the accident of the stock price going down, they are now putting out a high yield. So you always want to keep an eye out for these.

Or, maybe you already own a good dividend paying stock and its price goes down. So you might buy more stock in this case, if you feel the company is still a solid performer. So now your overall yield is even higher for all the stocks that you own. That's because your average cost for all of your stocks is now lower. This is actually called "averaging down."

So when others become afraid, you see an opportunity. Like that lemons to lemonade thing. You know, the old phrase that says when the world hands you lemons, turn them into lemonade.

Here's a real-world example of making lemonade for you. It's one of the best dividend stock investments I ever made, which happened during the big market downturn of 2008 - 2009.

It was with a company called MarkWest Energy Partners (MWE). I write about them in the past tense because they were taken over by another company and I no longer hold them. But back then, MarkWest was in the natural gas transport business and they owned a lot of natural gas pipelines.

And for every thousand cubic feet of natural gas that flowed through their pipelines, they charged a fee. Day in, day out, they got paid as other companies used their pipelines to move their natural gas to market. And they got paid the same whether the price of natural gas went up or went down.

Note that I think of MarkWest as a "stock-like" investment. Technically it's a Master Limited Partnership to be exact, not an individual stock like we've used in other examples. But for our purposes, it trades just like a dividend stock. It has a symbol like a stock. You can buy and sell like a stock. And it pays dividends (actually called distributions in this case) like a dividend stock. So to keep things simple, I'll just refer to it as a stock that is paying dividends.

By the way, these Master Limited Partnerships can be pretty profitable. They are required, by law, to pay you 90% of their profits. So their yields are often pretty good. I explain them and their profit potential for you in my future book entitled <u>**Make More Money With Special Stock-Like Investments.**</u>

And they had a pretty consistent record of increasing their dividends. Their typical dividend was around 6%, which was quite good. And during the crash of 2009, they kept their dividend the same and did not decrease it – which is saying a lot.

But during the crash, their price dropped extremely low. I looked at the company and their stock and thought, hey, this is still a good business. People are still going to use natural gas no matter what the market is doing. And these guys have miles and miles of pipelines that the industry must keep using. And what clinched it for me was when I figured you could sell the company, and its pipelines and other assets, for more than the total value of all of their shares of stock.

In other words, it was a good business selling at a deep discount.

So I bought a lot of shares. And it turned out that MarkWest was one of the best investment successes I've had. Because based on my purchase price, they were paying me a 20% dividend. I was collecting a $750 check every three months. And to add icing to the cake, the stock ultimately went back up 280%.

So that's a great advantage of dividend paying stocks. When the market goes down, they can often give you the opportunity to buy into some fat yields — and fat dividend paychecks.

They Keep Up With Inflation

Inflation is one of the biggest dangers to your secure retirement. This is because you lose purchasing power year after year. And the effect really adds up over time.

Just look at the chart below. Do you know that the dollar has lost over 40% of its purchasing power since 2000? And the dollar from 1900 to now is only worth about three cents. Wow! That's inflation for you. And you and I really need to pay attention to this. Especially as the Federal Reserve keeps printing trillions of dollars, with no end in sight.

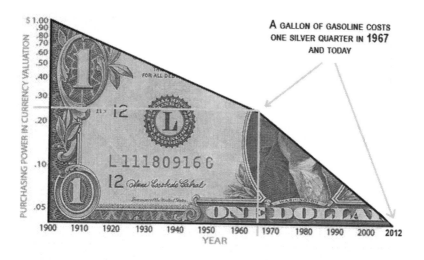

Figure 3-4. Purchasing Power Of The Dollar From 1900 To Present

So you may start your retirement with adequate funding in your retirement account. But unless you have some type of built in increase to cover the effects of inflation, eventually you are going to come up short when it's time to pay the bills. Because your bills are just going to keep going up. So your income needs to grow just to keep up.

I use an estimate of 3-4% a year for inflation. Of course, as I write this, inflation is much lower than that. But the Federal Reserve is trying to raise infla-

NO INFLATION HERE: Here's an interesting fact for you. While inflation has taken its toll in terms of the purchasing power of the dollar, it has not moved in terms of silver. In 1967, when quarters had 90% silver, you could buy a gallon of gasoline for one quarter.

Today, the silver in that quarter will buy you that same gallon of gasoline. So in terms of silver, if it was the currency, there is no inflation. To learn more preserving your wealth and silver investing, you can check out my book **Silver Investing For Beginners.**

tion as we speak. And historically, inflation has averaged about 3-4% a year. So that means any investment I want to use to fund my retirement needs to make at least that to keep up with the loss of purchasing power.

And this is the power of dividend paying stocks. There are plenty of them that increase their dividends by 3-4%. Which means your investments keep up with inflation.

But I go even better, and look for dividend stocks that increase their dividend by 7 - 12% a year. Now we're talking. Because not only will you keep up with inflation, but you will surpass it. You will GAIN purchasing power, year by year. And these gains are cumulative too.

For example, Microsoft (MSFT) has been increasing their dividend by 12% a year. Wow. That's about four times the average inflation rate. And there are other stocks that surpass the inflation rate as well.

This inflation beating aspect of good dividend paying stocks is one of their greatest features.

They Keep Management Honest And Frugal

Having to pay dividends to you on a regular basis keeps a company's top management more honest and frugal. This is because your dividends are paid out in cash. So the CEO has to make sure they have the cash to pay them.

And those cash payments make it harder to play tricks with the company's accounting. Because you have to keep coming up with real cash money to pay those pesky dividends. Investors are counting on them.

Which means the CEO has to keep the company running well and creating real profits.

Because there are many ways a CEO can manipulate earnings with their accounting. For example, they can make earnings look higher by arbitrarily booking a lower depreciation expense. That will make earnings look higher.

But that doesn't do anything for the cash situation. The earnings are higher but the cash is the same. After you deduct all the hard expenses from the real income, you still have the same amount of cash. Put another way, **earnings are a matter of opinion, but dividends PAID TO YOU are a matter of fact!** So dividend payments keep management's feet to the fire for more accurate financial reporting. It keeps them more honest.

And that's good for you.

Additionally, having to pay cash dividends also keeps them more frugal. So they're less inclined to go out and waste that hard-earned cash on foolish acquisitions.

Let's face it, CEO's are people too. And they have all of the same money temptations that other people have. For example, many profitable companies have accumulated a huge stash of cash. Like Microsoft, which has around $92 billion in cash on hand. And Apple even more, at $216 billion. And with all that cash laying around, it's tempting to just spend it on something foolish.

Apparently that was the case with Quaker Oats back in 1994. They purchased Snapple for $1.7 billion, looking for a brand-name to complement to their Gatorade line.

But the deal was a failure. Within three years they sold off Snapple to Triarc Beverages for just $300 million. That was a waste of $1.4 billion of stockholder money that left people scratching their heads. That money clearly would have been better spent by returning it to the stockholders as dividends.

It's kind of like the stories you read about lottery winners. People tend to do stupid things when they come into a big windfall of cash. About 70% of lottery winners who win big will go broke within a few years.

Why? Because they will foolishly spend the money, usually by giving away too much to friends.

So having to pay dividends quarter after quarter helps take some of that temptation away, and keeps management more focused on what is good for the stockholders.

It's not a guarantee, of course. But it helps. And that gives investing in good dividend paying stocks yet another edge.

And that is good for you as a dividend stock investor.

Take the bankruptcy of Enron, for example. Their stockholders were destroyed as the stock dropped from $90.56 a share to virtually nothing. And their employee's pensions were wiped out by the financial disaster as well. As best I can tell, (and it's complicated) Enron was borrowing money, and then booking it as revenue. Which made their earnings higher. It made them look profitable.

But borrowed money has to be paid back. It's not revenue. It's a loan. So that's a great example of a company manipulating earnings. Interestingly, Enron DID NOT pay a dividend. Because it's hard to keep paying a dividend if a company is running a complete fraud.

You can read a fascinating account of the Enron story here at https://en.wikipedia.org/wiki/Enron.

Uncomplicated Retirement Withdrawal

One of the nice things about dividend stocks is how easy it is to visualize your retirement income with them. You know what dividend paying stocks you own. And you know how much of a dividend they will pay you every month or quarter. So those are your retirement paychecks.

It's that simple.

Remember how we talked about some of the old, stable dividend stocks like AT&T? And how they have been called widow and orphan stocks in the past. This is what they were talking about. That families could invest in these dividend stocks. And count on the dividend checks to support the family if the wage earner, sadly, passed away.

Similarly, you can think of them as retirement stocks. And count on the dividend checks to help support you in retirement.

Here's a simple example. Let's say you own 3125 shares of AT&T (T) stock, and it pays a dividend of $1.92 a share per year. Then you will get $6000 per year (3125 X $1.92 = $6000.00), or $500 per month in dividends. That's your retirement income from that one stock. And that's pretty straightforward to figure out, don't you think?

Contrast that simplicity to the more typical retirement withdrawal scheme. Here you have to sell a portion of your stocks (and other investments) every month for your retirement income. Which means you constantly have to decide which ones to sell.

Every month you need income so you have to sell some. Even if the market is down. So you may have to sell them at too low of a price. And more frustrating, you realized you missed the higher price just a month ago. These are all the headaches of speculation and timing the market.

There are entire books written about retirement draw down methods. They go further into all kinds of formulas about how much you can draw down your account based on life expectancy. And assumptions and projections about stock and bond market performance. And many more factors too complicated to go into here.

But with dividend stocks you don't have to agonize over selling anything. You just keep getting the dividend checks. And living off of them.

Now don't just rush out and convert everything to dividend paying stocks. I can't advise you based on your unique situation. You should always discuss this with a qualified financial advisor. After all, it's your retirement, and future. So be careful with it.

But isn't it much easier to visualize your retirement checks with dividend stocks? And the dividends they will pay you.

I think so. So that's yet another advantage they give you.

4

KEY DATES FOR YOUR BIG PAYDAY

One of the most important dates you'll want to know is when you'll get paid. After all, this is why we invest in dividend paying stocks.

And there are other key dates you'll want to know as well. For example, companies pay their dividends over different time periods and frequencies. But they all tend to fall into these four time frames.

- Monthly

- Quarterly

- Annual

- Special Distributions

The most common payment frequency is quarterly – every three months. The second most common is monthly. We'll explore the different frequencies and dates in this section. And how you'll be notified of a pending dividend check. And when you need to own the stock in order to qualify for your dividend check.

Some Companies Pay Monthly Just Like A Paycheck

While most companies pay on a quarterly basis, there are quite a few that pay monthly. Monthly distributions have a special appeal because they really feel like paychecks. Every month, like clockwork, you get that dividend check in the mail.

Of the roughly 3000 dividend paying stocks in the US, my recent count showed that 752 pay monthly. So that's a pretty big list to choose from. You can find this list at http://www.dividend.com/dividend-stocks/monthly-dividend-stocks.php.

Personally, I own a few monthly dividend stocks. But most of my holdings are in quarterly dividend paying stocks. Now, I love the monthly paying stocks. And my monthly stocks seem to have higher dividends too. But the quarterly dividend stocks seem to have higher dividend increases than the monthly stocks.

So not only am I getting their quarterly paychecks, but I am getting bigger raises each year. Which means my dividend checks grow faster year over year. And another advantage of quarterly paying stocks is that you have a bigger list to choose from.

So what you choose is a tradeoff. It really comes down to your personal financial goals. And where you are in life at this point. For example, if you are retired, and relying heavily on your stocks for income, you may prefer more monthly dividend stocks in your portfolio. If you are not retired yet, and still growing the value of your portfolio, and dividends, at the fastest possible rate, then quarterly may be the way to go.

Or you can do a mix like I do. It's really up to you.

A couple of monthly dividend stocks I have owned through the years are Calamos Convertible & High Income Fund (CHY) and American Capital Agency Corp (AGNC).

Calamos pays a whopping 10.67% dividend. And American Capital Agency an even better 11.24%. So you can see their appeal. And even better, as I said, they pay monthly.

As of this writing I currently own Calamos, but not American Capital Agency. But you might consider adding both of them to your future buy list, for when their stock price becomes attractive.

And then there are some companies that pay dividends once a year. I don't recall ever owning any of these. Perhaps I'm too impatient. I like to see my dividend checks rolling in more frequently.

However, there are some companies that pay out quarterly, and then they pay an extra dividend at the end of the year. I've owned a few of these. And the extra dividend at the end of the year is like getting a bonus. So these stocks are like getting paychecks, raises and a BONUS. That's not hard to take at all. But by and large, you'll not find as many of these to invest in.

And finally, there are special distributions. These happen when some special circumstances arise. For example, Microsoft did a whopping special distribution back in 2004 of $3.08 a share. Compare that to their normal $.08 a share at the time. Microsoft had a huge $60 billion cash hoard at the time. So they were pressured by stockholders to share some of it.

That special distribution looked like this.

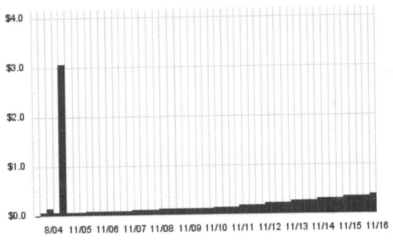

Figure 4-1. What A Special Dividend Looks Like – Microsoft (MSFT)
Image courtesy of www.DividendChannel.com

Imagine what a nice surprise that was for Microsoft stockholders. That said, these are special situations that don't happen that often. So you can't really count on them. I tend to think of them as extra gravy. But that's some kind of gravy.

So overall, you will focus on quarterly and monthly dividend paying stocks. And to keep things simple, I mainly refer to quarterly payments throughout the book. But just be aware there are monthly dividend payments. And annual and special distributions too.

Of course, for you alert readers, there are a few stocks that pay semi-annual dividends. But these are rare. One of them is Barclays, a holding company with subsidiaries in global financial services including retail banking, credit cards, etc.

While they still pay a dividend, it looks like they cut it substantially back in 2008. So it doesn't look like an interesting dividend stock to me. I just list it here as an example of one of the few stocks that pays dividends semi-annually.

So that covers the time frames when you will be paid. But there are some other important dates for you to be aware of.

Your Big Payday - The Dividend Announcement

So how does your dividend payment happen? What are the events that lead up to a check in your mailbox?

Well, there are a number of key dates you need to be aware of. So we'll look into them. But before we do, a word of encouragement. If you are a long-term investor in the stock, you don't really need to worry about any of them. This will all happen automatically for you.

That said, here's what happens to get you your dividend check. Every three months, the board of directors of the company will announce a dividend. The day they announce this is called the **"announcement date,"** or the "declaration date." And once this dividend is authorized, the company has a legal liability to pay it.

Here is a typical dividend announcement. You are most interested in the parts I have bolded. They are, the amount of the dividend, and two other key dates.

Microsoft Declares Quarterly Dividend
Posted December 3, 2014 By Microsoft News Center
REDMOND, Wash. — Dec. 3, 2014 — Microsoft Corp. on Wednesday announced that its board of directors declared a quarterly **dividend of $0.31 per share**. The dividend is **payable March 12, 2015**, to shareholders of record on Feb. 19, 2015. The **ex-dividend date will be Feb. 17, 2015.**

So looking at the announcement, you see that it says the **"ex-dividend date will be Feb. 17, 2015."** That's very important and here's what it means to you. If you own the stock on February 16, the day before the ex-dividend date, you will be paid the dividend. If you wait until February 17 (the ex-dividend date) to buy the stock, you will not be paid that specific quarterly dividend.

So the big takeaway here is to not sell your stock before the ex-dividend date if you want to get the dividend. You want to own the stock on the day before the ex-dividend date (February 16) in order to get the dividend check.

For those of you interested in word origins and Latin, the prefix "ex" means "not" or "without" in this context. So ex-dividend means "without" dividend. So those that don't buy the stock until the ex-dividend means they buy it "without" the dividend, i.e. they don't get the dividend for this quarter.

So the most important date for you to pay attention to is the ex-dividend date. Because this is the date that determines if you get paid. And that's why we are invested in dividend stocks in the first place.

So that we can get paid.

Which leads us to the other key date, the **"payable date."** In our example above you would get paid your Microsoft dividend on March 12. Good to know, yes?

And they also tell you the amount of the dividend - in this case $.31 for every share of stock you own. So if you own 100 shares of Microsoft, you will receive a $31 check in the mail. Or if you own 1000 shares, you will get a $310 check.

So those are the key pieces of information to be aware of...

- The **Amount of the Dividend** - in this case $.31 per share.
- The **Announcement Date** - December 3 in this example.
- The **Ex-Dividend Date** - February 17 - be sure and own the stock the day before.
- The **Payable Date** - March 12 - check is mailed to you - *Oh Happy Day!*

Again, remember that you don't have to do anything for this to happen, outside of making sure you own the stock the day before the ex-dividend date. All of this will happen automatically.

Which is why I call these dividend paying stocks "set it and forget it." And what's not to like about that?

Harvesting Dividends - Dividend Capture

Thinking about the key dates in the last chapter, you may have zeroed in on the ex-dividend date. Recall that you must own the stock the day before this date to get the dividend.

And you may have thought, *hey, I see where I can make a lot of money here.* I can just buy stocks right before the ex-dividend date, collect the dividend, then sell the stocks the next day, and go buy some different stocks just before their ex-dividend dates. And collect their dividends. Over and over again. Rinse and repeat.

And in fact, you can do this. There is nothing to stop you. And in theory, this sounds like a great idea. There's actually a name for this practice. It's called "dividend capture" or "harvesting dividends."

But in practice, actually doing dividend capture is a controversial topic. It's not controversial because it's wrong to do, or anything like that. But just that there's no consensus that this actually works.

The main drawback to this idea is that the value of a stock typically drops on the ex-dividend date - the day you would sell it. And it drops by about the amount of the dividend that will be paid. So when you sell the stock, you will sell it at a loss of about the same amount you gained capturing the dividend. So you net out to zero.

This is because the current stock buyers you are selling to realize they will not get the most recently announced dividend. So they are not willing to pay as much for the stock.

Three months later they will likely buy it from you at a higher price, because they know they will get the next dividend. But you want to own it then too, so you can get the next dividend. So this defeats the purpose of the dividend capture strategy altogether.

Additionally, by churning through all of these transactions to capture more dividends, you are going to be paying additional commissions on them. That can eat into any slim dividend profit you can theoretically make. And there are tax implications as well, based on how long you have held a stock. And those may cost you even more.

So there may be instances where people are successful at dividend capture. I won't rule that out. But it seems like a lot of work to me - for little or no pay-off. Which flies in the face of one of the benefits of dividend paying stocks. And that is their easy, set it and forget it benefit.

If I'm going to spend extra effort like this, it seems more productive to research and find the next great dividend stock I can buy. Or check up on the ones I have, to make sure they are doing okay. Or see if there is one I can replace with a better one.

So I just buy good dividend paying stocks, and collect the dividends. And kick back and don't try anything fancy like this. I know the price will probably go down right after the ex-dividend date. And it will gradually come back up as time passes to the next dividend announcement.

And I leave it at that. What could be simpler?

5

HOW TO FIND GOOD DIVIDEND STOCKS TO BUY

Choosing good dividend stocks to invest in is the most important thing you will do. Because some dividend stocks are much better than others. So how can you recognize a good dividend stock?

Well, there are some simple clues you'll learn to look for in this section. They are...

- Does the stock actually pay a dividend?
- Has it consistently paid a dividend?
- Has it consistently raised the dividend?
- Is the dividend / increase big enough?
- Can it keep paying the dividend?

And here's the good news. You don't need to do all kinds of complicated analysis to figure this out. In fact, there is a very simple way to avoid most of this effort. And that is to just get the research done for you.

How do you do that? By subscribing to an investment newsletter or two. They do the work. You buy the stocks they recommend. And then you are back in set it and forget it mode.

I'll share a couple of excellent newsletters with you at the end of this section. And as of this writing, I subscribe to both of them. They are that good. Especially when you consider that I can, and often do, my own analysis.

But if you are so inclined, it's good to do some of your own research as well. So I suggest you at least read though this section. Because it's good to know what makes a good dividend paying stock. This will help you choose them if you want to do the research yourself. Or help you appreciate what the newsletters are doing for you if you don't.

Knowing this will put you way ahead of the typical stock investor. And help keep those paychecks and raises coming, quarter after quarter, year after year.

Does It Pay A Dividend?

The first thing to check out is if the stock you're considering actually pays a dividend. And this information is easy to find.

For example, you can check this quickly at www.Yahoo.com. Just go to the Yahoo site and then click on Finance on the left-hand side of the screen. Then enter the stock symbol in the search box at the top, and click the Search button.

NOTE: If you don't know the stock symbol, just enter the company name in the same box, and press the Symbol Lookup link below it. It will come back with a list of stocks with that name in it, and their symbols. Then just click on the company you're looking for and it will show you their Symbol, and look the information up for you.

For example, take Sysco, the restaurant and grocery distributor. It's one of my favorite stocks. To check if Sysco (SYY) pays a dividend, enter their stock symbol SYY into the search box and click the Search button. In the information displayed, you will see a line like this.

Dividend & Yield   1.24 (2.33%)

This means that Sysco DOES indeed pay a dividend. The dividend it pays is $1.24 per share. And that means it is paying you a 2.33% yield if you bought it right now at the current price.

Stocks that do not pay a dividend will show something like this.

Dividend & Yield   N/A (N/A)

Which means dividend information is Not Applicable, i.e. the stock does not pay a dividend.

You can also find this out in your stockholder account. Just use the search function for the stock symbol, and then look at the information that comes back.

For example, using TDAmeritrade, I can also check out Sysco. And just like above, I enter the stock symbol SYY into the Symbols Box in the upper right-hand part of the screen. Then I press the Search button. And it comes back with all kinds of information about Sysco stock, including this...

- **Annual Dividend - $1.24**

- **Dividend Yield - 2.33%**

Just like Yahoo, this tells me that Sysco does indeed pay a dividend. And they will pay me $1.24 per year for every share that I own (Annual Dividend). That will give me a 2.33% return on my money (Dividend Yield) at the current stock price.

So we have confirmed that Sysco (SYY) is indeed a dividend paying stock. So that's a good start. Now, on to the next important question. And that is, have they consistently paid a dividend?

Have They Consistently Paid A Dividend?

Remember, the dividends from the stock you are checking out are going to be your paychecks. So you would like to get them on a regular basis, right?

So we want to look at the dividend paying history of this company and make sure they have paid their dividend, quarter after quarter, without interruption.

To do this, we research their dividend history. And you can find that information at this great dividend site - https://www.dividendchannel.com/.

When you go to the site you will enter the stock symbol in the box at the top that says Enter Symbol. Then press the Get Quote & Dividend History button next to that. Then, looking at the right-hand side of the page, scroll down until you come to a column called DIVIDEND HISTORY.

Again, looking up Sysco (SYY), you will see something like this...

Dividend History

Date	Div
06/29/16	0.310
03/30/16	0.310
01/06/16	0.310
09/30/15	0.300
06/30/15	0.300
03/31/15	0.300
12/30/14	0.300
10/01/14	0.290
07/01/14	0.290
04/02/14	0.290
12/31/13	0.290
10/02/13	0.280

Each row shows the date the quarterly dividend was paid. And it shows how much the dividend was. In this example, the last dividend paid was $.31 a share on 06/29/16. So if you owned 100 shares, your quarterly dividend check would be for $31. If you owned 1000 shares, it would be for $310.

Looking at the dates paid, you can see that they have paid every three months. And there aren't any missing payments either. So that's a really good sign. Also note that the screen actually shows their paid quarterly dividends all the way back to 1996, I just shortened the list for this book.

Now, if they have paid consistently, but maybe missed a payment or so during the Great Recession of 2008, I may overlook that. On the other hand, if they still kept making payments during that time, that's terrific. It means these folks are serious about paying their dividend. And indeed, Sysco kept paying their dividend through that challenging time. So that's a good thing.

That said, I tend to focus most on what has happened in the past 5 years, because the current history is the most telling for making an investment decision today. But a longer history is even better. Because it reaffirms that they are a solid stock to invest in.

So now we know that the stock has paid dividends consistently. And we can feel assured that our paychecks will probably keep coming in on a regular basis. So this stock has passed our second test.

Now, on to the next test. And that is, "Have they been **increasing** the dividend year after year?" Because these are our future raises.

Have They Consistently Raised Their Dividend?

Companies that consistently raise their dividend are sending out a big clue that they are...

- Well managed

- Profitable

- Confident in their future

- Are good dividend stocks for you to invest in

This is where things get exciting for you. Because not only will you be getting checks from them, but you'll be getting raises too. And who doesn't get excited about raises.

Put another way, the company is doing so well that they are growing their profits. And they will be sharing that growth with you as an investor, as one of their owners.

So how do we check this important fact out?

Well, we go back to the https://www.dividendchannel.com/ web site. And look up the stock symbol as we described before. Then, looking at the middle of the screen, scroll down until you see a chart, called DIVIDEND HISTORY CHART. In the case of Sysco (SYY) you will see something like this...

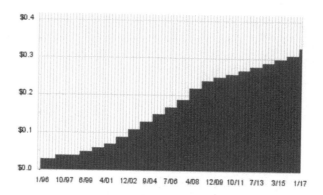

Figure 5-1. What Excellent Dividend Increases Look Like – Sysco (SYY)
Image courtesy of www.DividendChannel.com

This chart shows the annual dividend per share that has been paid, year by year. And Sysco's chart, shown above, is just what you are looking for. It's clear that Sysco has been raising their dividend every year.

The chart looks like a staircase, right? Like your staircase to financial success. That's what it looks like to me.

Now again, sometimes you will see a chart where the dividend didn't increase around the years 2008 - 2009 because of the great recession. But if they have increased their dividend before and after that, I might still be interested. Because many companies were just fighting to survive.

On the other hand, if they kept increasing their dividend during that challenging time, they get extra points. Because that is truly exceptional performance.

But overall, I look for increases in years 2010 and beyond. Because most good dividend paying stocks were able to recover by then, and start increasing their dividend again.

So increasing dividends is a key test of most good dividend paying stocks. And with one exception, which we'll get into later, I won't invest unless they pass this test.

HOW'S 25 YEARS FOR A GREAT TRACK RECORD? As of this writing there are 51 companies that have raised their dividend every year for the last twenty-five years. That's an outstanding performance by any measure!

So outstanding in fact, that these stocks are called the Dividend Aristo-crats. This is a great list to start looking for good dividend paying stocks. And you can see them listed here at https://investorjunkie.com/3974/dividend-aristocrats/. Or just go to Google and search for "List of dividend aristocrats."

Favor Strong Dividend Growers If Possible

I tend to favor dividend stocks that have a higher dividend growth rate. Be-cause these are your raises. So I look for stocks that have been raising their dividend by 8 - 12% a year. This really begins to add up, year over year. And before you know it, a stock that originally paid you 3% in dividends will be paying you 10% based on your original purchase price.

For example, take a stock that pays a 3% dividend and increases its dividend by 10% each year. By year 5, that dividend will have grown to 4.4% to your original purchase price. By year 10, it's yielding 7.1%. And by year 15, a whopping 11.4%.

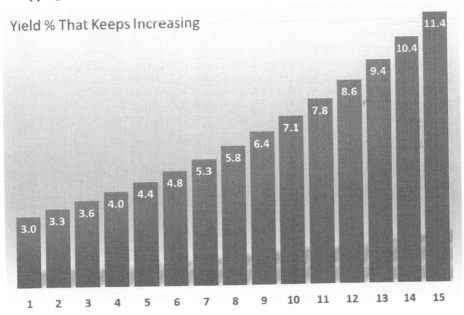

Figure 5-2. A 3% Yield Increasing By 10% Per Year

And all you had to do was buy it, and then let it grow, year by year. No extra effort required.

Now, as a general rule, stocks you buy that have a high dividend growth rate will tend to have a lower dividend. And stocks you buy that have a higher dividend will tend to have a lower, or no, growth rate. Like in our example above, where the dividend started out at 3% but grew by 10% a year. Contrast this to a stock or fund that has an immediate 10% dividend, but only grows at 1% a year, or no growth at all.

So if you are already retired, you may favor buying more of the higher yield, lower growth rate stocks. Because they will immediately be paying you a bigger paycheck. However, you might still throw some big growers into the mix. Because this will help you keep up with inflation.

If, on the other hand, you have a longer time horizon, it's probably better to go for more of the higher growth rate / lower yield stocks. But here again, you might throw in a few high dividend, lower growth stocks. Because this will get more investment money flowing into your account right away.

So this is really about what mix of these two types of dividend stocks you choose. It's not necessarily just a flat-out decision to buy one or the other. And since everyone's situation is different, you will need to make that decision.

How To Get The Dividend Growth Rate

At this point we've seen that growth rate is important to your investing decision. So how do you find out what the dividend growth rate is?

Well, you find it by using one of these three ways…

- Find it in a pre-calculated list

- Find it at the company's web site

- Calculate it

The easiest way is to find it is in a pre-calculated list if possible. And the best list I have found is at http://dripinvesting.org. If you click in the Info/Tools/

Forms section of the site it will take you to the Drip Investing Resource Center page.

Click on the http://www.tessellation.com/david_fish/ link and download the most recent spreadsheet. This spreadsheet will have pre-calculated the dividend growth rate of more than 750 dividend paying stocks. They are all shown in one list under the CCC tab (which stands for Champions, Contenders and Challengers).

Just scroll down to the stock you are looking for. And then scroll to the right, where you will see columns saying DGR (Dividend Growth Rate). These columns will show you the growth rate for different time periods, like three years, five years, etc. And they exclude any special dividends, which is a good thing. Because excluding these shows what you can typically expect for dividend growth.

Stocks showing a 3-5 year growth rate of around 10% are of particular interest here. That's because this is an exceptional growth of your dividends. Again, remember that this is showing you your future raises in our paychecks and raises analogy.

So finding the growth rate in a pre-calculated list is best if your stock is on the list.

But if you can't find it that way, it should be on the company's web site. Just go to their site and look under Investor Relations, or some tab to that effect. Companies with a consistent and strong dividend growth rate will be proud to brag about their dividend growth rate. And they have every right to brag about it in my opinion. Because this is a real accomplishment.

If you can't find the growth rate anywhere, then you can calculate it. To do this, the first thing you need is the dividend history, i.e. how much dividend the company paid each year. A good site to find this history is at http://www.dividendchannel.com/. Just search on the stock symbol once you are at the site, and you will see the dividend history. You will usually see five to ten years listed, which is plenty.

Then you simply calculate the increase for each year to the next. And you average those increase percents. For example, let's say ABC Company had the following three-year dividend history.

2013: $1.00
2014: $1.10
2015: $1.25

Looking at 2014, you can see it had a 10% increase from 2013 (1.10-1.00=.10, 10/100=10%) and 2015 had a 13.6% increase (1.25-1.10=.15 and 15/110=13.6%).

So then you average these two increase percent's (10% + 13.6% / 2 years increases) which gives you 11.8% average increase over the last two years.

So that's how you can calculate the dividend growth rate if you can't find it in a pre-calculated list or the investor relations section of the company's web site. Of course, a good financial newsletter will always tell you this important number too.

Can They Keep Paying The Dividend?

So you've learned at this point that a great dividend stock consistently pays a dividend, and increases it. But can they keep doing it? That's the big question.

This is important to you because you don't want your checks to suddenly stop in the future. You want them to keep coming, showing up in your mailbox, quarter after quarter, year after year.

So how do you check this out?

Well, there are a couple of ways. One is to simply look at their past performance. And the other is to look at their finances to understand their ability to pay. Kind of like how credit card companies look at your ability to pay.

Looking at their past performance is the simplest way to do this. Actually, that's what we just did in the last two chapters. We saw that Sysco has paid a dividend consistently year over year. And that they've been consistently increasing it.

So while past performance is no guarantee of future results, it can be a good indication. And it's a pretty good bet that Sysco will keep paying their dividend in the future. Or as Mark Twain is reputed to have said, "History doesn't repeat itself, but it often rhymes."

So if you just do this simple check before you invest, you will be way ahead of most stock investors.

But it's good to go even further with this if you can. And look at their financial performance to get a clue if they are making enough money to keep paying their dividends. The way we do this is to look at how much money they make, compared to how much they pay out in dividends.

For example, if good company ABC has made $10 million in profits, and paid out $5 million in dividends, they are only paying out half of their profits. So they can probably keep doing this, year after year.

On the other hand, if bad company XYZ has made $10 million in profits, but they paid out $11 million in dividends, they are paying out more than their profits. So they simply can't keep doing this, year after year. Something is going to have to give.

They can't keep **covering** that dividend with the money they make. They can't keep making that **payou**t, year after year.

So you can see that the ratio between those two numbers is very important. And if we divide how much they **paid out** by how much they made, we get something called a **payout ratio**, or a **coverage ratio** (we'll use the term payout ratio going forward, i.e. they can keep paying out that dividend to you).

And that ratio, that one number, will tell us what we need to know.

Figuring out the payout ratio looks like this. Money Paid / Money Made = Payout Ratio. So let's compare our two companies.

ABC Company: $5M Money Paid / $10 Money Made = **.50 Payout Ratio**

XYZ Company: $11M Money Paid / $10M Money Made = **1.10 Payout Ratio**

The ABC Company, with a payout ratio of .50, is only paying out half of their money made. So, like we said, they can probably keep doing that. So a ratio of .50 is a good thing.

But XYZ Company, with a payout ratio of 1.10, is paying out more than they are making. They can't keep doing that for long. We can say a ratio of 1.10 is a bad thing.

Dividend Yield	Annualized Payout	Payout Ratio	Dividend Growth
2.49%	$1.24	53.4%	45 yrs

Figure 5-3. Payout Ratio

So here's a general rule of thumb for you. **You want to invest in companies whose payout ratio is not greater than .70.** Because that means they are paying out less than they are making, and have money left over. That money left over gives you a bit of a cushion to assure your dividend checks will keep coming.

So how do you find out the payout ratio? Here's an easy way for you. Just go to the website http://www.dividend.com/dividend-stocks/. Then enter the stock symbol in the search box at the top and click. For example, if you search SYY (Sysco), you will see something like this.

See where Sysco is paying out 53.4% of their profits? That's about half, like our good company ABC at .50. And 53.4 is less than our .70 payout ratio rule of thumb. So Sysco definitely passes the test. The odds are good they can keep paying their dividend.

HOW ANALYSTS CALCULATE THE PAYOUT RATIO: I don't expect you to do this, because it gets a little bit involved. But for those interested, here's how the analysts research the payout ratio. To start with, it's easy to say just divide the Money Made by the Money Paid. But the trick is finding out those two numbers.

And to do this you have to look at the financial statements of the company in question. Of course, you can just look at the Income Statement of the company and see if they continue to be profitable year over year.

But Income Statements can be jiggered a bit. So the real gold standard is to look at the company's Cash Flow Statement. That's because it's harder to jigger the cash position. So using the cash flow number, you are looking to see if the company brings in more cash each year than they pay out in dividends.

To determine the dividend payout, you multiply the annual dividend X the total number of shares outstanding. That will tell you the total amount of dividends that will be paid out. That's the Money /Paid.

Then you look at the company's Cash Flow Analysis. The bottom line will show you how much cash they have left after they have paid all of their expenses. That's the Money Made. Now you can divide the Money Paid by the Money Made.

If they have more cash than dividends paid, then yes, they will probably be able to pay the dividend. But as mentioned before, you want them to have even MORE cash than dividend payments. This provides you with a safety margin. And a good margin is a payout ratio not greater than .70.

So that's how easy it is to check out the payout ratio before you invest.

Of course, if you subscribe to financial newsletters like I mention later in the book, it's even easier, as they do this payout ratio check for you.

Is The Dividend And Increase Worth It?

Since you are investing your hard-earned money into a dividend stock, you want to make sure the whole exercise is worth your while. That is to say, that you'll get big enough dividends - your paychecks. And big enough raises through dividend increases.

After all, you probably wouldn't work for $1 an hour, with a job that only gave a .01% increase. This simply would not be worth your time and effort. Ditto for dividend stocks. You want them to pay you a worthwhile dividend and get a meaningful increase year after year.

So what's good? Well, I would say a dividend around 3% with increases around 10% per year is a good benchmark, a good starting point. But it

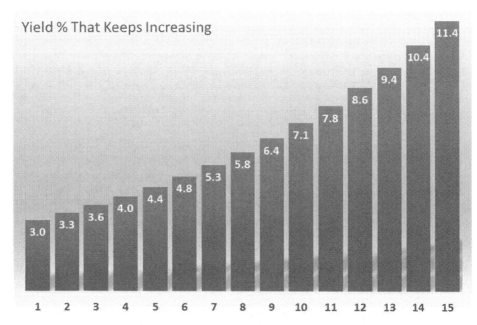

Figure 5-4. A 3% Yield Increasing By 10% Per Year

doesn't have to be this exactly. I just used these numbers as a guideline. A strong stock paying 2.5% with a dividend increase from 6% to 11% a year could be good as well. Or a stock that pays 4.5% with a lower percent increase might be good.

But I always start with the 3% now/10% increase idea when I'm evaluating a stock - and go from there.

Here's what that would look like over time. We've looked at this before but it bears repeating.

Year 1 shows the stock paying 3%. Then in year 2 the dividend is raised by 10% (3% X 1.10 = 3.4%). So now it is paying you 3.4%, based on your original purchase price. So if you just do nothing, and hang on to this stock, by year 6 it is paying you over 5%, and by year 12, a fat 10.4%.

MSFT	35 a share		1.12		
Year	Invest	Yield %	Check	Total Dividends	
1	3500	3	$105.00	$105.00	
2	3500	3.4	$117.60	$222.60	
3	3500	3.8	$131.71	$354.31	
4	3500	4.2	$147.52	$501.83	
5	3500	4.7	$165.22	$667.05	
6	3500	5.3	$185.05	$852.09	
7	3500	5.9	$207.25	$1,059.35	
8	3500	6.6	$232.12	$1,291.47	
9	3500	7.4	$259.98	$1,551.44	
10	3500	8.3	$291.17	$1,842.62	
11	3500	9.3	$326.11	$2,168.73	
12	3500	10.4	$365.25	$2,533.98	
13	3500	11.7	$409.08	$2,943.06	
14	3500	13.1	$458.17	$3,401.22	
15	3500	14.7	$513.15	$3,914.37	

Figure 5-5. Real World Microsoft Investment

And you were collecting all of those dividends at increasing rates along the way. So this type of dividend stock is definitely worth your while.

Here's a real-world example for you. I invested in MSFT a few years ago at $35 a share. And Microsoft's dividend increase is around 12% a year. So if you made a 100 share investment, here's how that would grow over time.

Just look at the running total of the dividends in Total Dividend column. By year 14, Microsoft has paid almost all of my original investment back to me - just in dividends. In other words, the stock bought itself for me. So from then on, all the dividend money is free.

I love free money, don't you?

Also, by year fourteen, my checks are 4 1/2 times larger than they were when I started out. Wouldn't you like that kind of raise on the job.

Just think about it. If you take the average salary in America of $50,000 a year, that means in 14 years you would be making $225,000 per year. This is particularly interesting since the average salary of American workers has actually declined over the past 15 years. And in some demographic groups, actually declined by as much as 25%.

And I didn't even mention how much faster my investment would grow if I reinvested the dividends (we get into that later). And I didn't mention that Microsoft has now gone up from $35 to $56 a share, giving me an additional $2100 profit ($56 a share - $35 a share X 100 shares).

So dividends might start out small and slow, but over time they can become quite large. The real key here is how fast the dividend increases - in this case 12%. So I tend to favor higher increases versus a higher initial dividend.

So if I was considering a stock that paid 2.5% but had a dividend increase of 12%, I would probably favor it over a stock that has a dividend of 4.5% with a dividend increase of 4%. Because I know the dividend will grow faster, catch up, and pass the 4.5% dividend stock.

Now there are a couple of exceptions to this. One is where you are already in retirement, and you need some of your stocks to pay a maximum dividend right now. Then you might favor a 10% dividend with a low or no dividend growth rate.

And these 10% stocks do exist. Government Properties (GOV) comes to mind - a stock I have invested in in the past. GOV is a company that buys properties and rents them to the government. Seems like a pretty secure business model, doesn't it? Because do you actually believe the government will quit renting properties - or cut their spending. Probably not. The government just keeps expanding, so if anything, they will continue to rent even more properties.

So if you need part of you stocks to generate maximum income, you can give up some growth to get more money now.

Conversely, one area where I do go for small dividends, AND probably low dividend growth, is in precious metals - specifically gold and silver. I like to hold gold and silver stocks in my portfolio for insurance, stability and safety.

Many precious metals stocks pay no dividend at all. So when I find a good company that pays any kind of dividend, I go for it. Royal Gold (RGLD), Silver Wheaton (SLW) and VanEck Vectors Junior Gold Miners ETF (GDXJ) all come to mind, and I hold, or have held, these stocks in the past.

By the way, I think it's important for most people to have some precious metals investments. And silver is one of the best to own. In my future book entitled <u>Silver Investing For Beginners - Invest In REAL Money Today For A Wealthier Future Tomorrow.</u> I share all the insights I've developed trading and investing in silver for over 30 years. And you can invest for just $3 to begin with. Even a child can use the $3 technique - and some do. Soon to be available in eBook format.

But those two exceptions aside, **try to shoot for the 3% dividend / 10% growth benchmark.** That way, your dividend stock investing will be worth your while. And after some years, you'll be pulling in some fat dividend checks in your mailbox.

A Final Gut Check

OK, so now you have done all of your due diligence. And let's say the stock you are considering has passed all the tests.

That's great! Now just do one final gut check before you get ready to buy it.

And the gut check is simple. It is, do you understand what the company does? And do you think there will be a continued demand for their products (or services) in the future? Because this is the only way they will continue to be profitable. And the only way they will continue to pay you dividends.

In other words, are they going to be around for a while?

Back to our Clorox example. Do you understand what Clorox does? I'll bet you do. Clorox makes bleach that you probably use when you wash your clothes. People have been washing their clothes with Clorox bleach since the company formed in 1913. And no matter what the economy does, people will keep washing their clothes in the future. And they will probably keep using Clorox.

Even if there is another recession, or worse yet, a depression, or the stock market tanks, people are going to keep washing their clothes. And Clorox will keep selling them bleach. So it's a pretty safe bet that Clorox will be able to keep paying you a dividend, don't you think?

Or another example, with Hershey, the chocolate bar producer. I'll bet you understand their product too. People have been buying Hershey chocolate bars for years. Since 1900, to be exact, when Milton S. Hershey began manufacturing Hershey's Milk Chocolate Bars. And people will keep buying Hershey chocolate for years to come. Even if there is a huge problem with the economy, they will keep buying chocolate bars - maybe more so than ever because they're depressed.

You see Hershey's chocolate bars at the grocery store checkout counter all of the time. And you see the bottles of Clorox in the detergent aisle of the grocery store every time you shop. Indeed, you see these so often you may not have even think of them. They are actually kind of boring.

And that's a good thing. Boring and familiar is beautiful when it comes to dividend paying stocks. Indeed, this is something Peter Lynch, one of the all-time great stock investors, has said. He buys stocks in products he knows - or products his family tells him about.

Ditto for Warren Buffett, probably the greatest investor of all time. He buys what he understands. And it's boring. So some of his major holdings are Coca-Cola, Gillette razors, and See's Candies.

Boring. Boring. Boring.

And beautiful.

Now all of your dividend stocks don't have to be boring. They can be more exciting like Apple or Microsoft. But the larger point here is to understand the company, and feel that they have a solid future ahead of them. And that people will keep buying their products. So you will keep getting your dividend checks.

And that's your final gut check before you buy.

Find Good Stocks The Easy Way - Dividend Newsletters

By now you understand the importance of choosing good dividend stocks to buy. And we've covered a number of ways to check them out.

However, if this seems like a lot of work to you, there is an easier way. And that is to have someone else do the research for you. I'm talking about paying for a subscription to a financial newsletter.

Now paying money for stock recommendations may be a new idea to you. It may even be something your brain kind of resists at first. But before you immediately rule it out, here's how it can work for you.

These newsletters typically come out monthly. And each issue will recommend a number of dividend stocks, or income producing investments. Their skilled analysts will have done all of the research we covered earlier. And they summarize this for you, describing the companies, the research they did, and their specific buy recommendations.

So all you do is just read the newsletter and their research. And if you like the recommendation, you can buy the stock. And feel good about it. Because you know the research has been done. So you've done your due diligence, by having someone else do it for you.

How easy is that?

And you may be surprised how inexpensive some newsletters are. And what a terrific value they can be for the money. For example, I typically buy newslet-

NEWSLETTER PRICES - YIKES: When it comes to newsletter prices, they can range from free to up to $25,000 per year and more. We'll be avoiding the $25,000 per year variety. The latter are more for institutions or very wealthy investors.

ters that cost around $60 to $89 per year. But they are often on sale for $39 per year if you catch their specials and introductory offers. That's about nine lattes per year at Starbucks. And these newsletters can make you some "green" bucks.

Here's another good reason to subscribe. Because by using a newsletter, you don't feel like you're out there all alone, just guessing. It's like the newsletter writers are kind of in there with you. Actually, they're very much focused on good recommendations for you, because they have a successful reputation to protect. So they can sell more newsletters.

Now there are literally hundreds of financial newsletters offered to the general public. And you could easily get lost in this publishing maze. So I'll keep it simple and just mention a couple of them later in this section, both around $50. And you hey might be right for you.

One final point. You may recall that I was a financial consultant and New York Stock Exchange licensed stockbroker in the past. So I could do this re-search myself. And back then, working for a large, national broker / dealer, I also had all kinds of free company research available to me.

And I still bought newsletters for myself. And these days, I continue to buy specific newsletters. And often, after doing a little checking, make many of my stock investments based on their recommendations.

In my opinion, they are that good.

What To Look For In A Good Newsletter

Not every financial newsletter out there is great or easy to use. But through the years I've zeroed in on newsletters that have a specific format. The format works for me, and it can be good for you too, especially if you are a beginning investor.

For example, the newsletter writer always tells a story about each recommen-dation they are making. They describe the research they did, and why they think the stock is a good investment. And they also discuss the risks and any other downsides that they considered.

Finally, they ALWAYS end the story with a specific buy statement that looks like this. Example*: **Buy Sprint (NYSE: S) up to $5 a share and use a 25% trailing stop.**

Here's why this is good for you. Even if you don't understand all of the analysis and research they describe in the story, you will know EXACTLY what to buy, and at what price, to take advantage of their recommendation.

In our example above, here's what they said about their Sprint recommendation.

- They told you to buy Sprint stock.

- They told you to not buy it for more than $5 a share.

- They told you what exchange the stock trades on (NYSE - the New York Stock Exchange).
- They told you the Stock symbol "S" (to use when placing your order).

- They even told you when to get out of the stock (25% trailing stop - we'll get into that later).

What could be more specific? And easier?

So if you are one of those people that skips to the back of a book to find out the ending, you could do the same here. You could just skip the story and analysis and look at the one-sentence buy recommendation. Then decide how many shares you want to buy, and place the order.

Now I really don't recommend that, because I think you'll begin to learn more about stocks as you read the stories. And even if you don't get the whole thing, you'll begin to understand more and more over time. Also, the stories are usually written in an interesting way.

I have some friends who don't know much about stocks at all. And I've shared some of these newsletter stories and recommendations with them. And they read them from top to bottom. They may not understand the whole thing, but they get the general idea. And you will too.

And it gets better. Because when you buy one of these newsletters, they will send you updates on how the stock is doing, and even special email alerts if the stock starts going bad.

So they do all the business research for you, thus saving you hours of work. And they tell you exactly what to buy and how much to pay. And they tell you when to get out.

Additionally, at the end of the newsletter, they have a list of all of their current recommendations, how they are doing, which ones you can still buy if you like, and the maximum price you should pay for them.

That pretty much covers everything you need to know, right?

I think you'll agree this is so much better than Uncle Harry's stock tip he tells you about at Thanksgiving after he's had a couple of drinks. Or the hot stock tip your buddy tells you about. Or the hot stock mentioned on the evening news. By the way, I've heard some of these newscasters can't even balance their expense accounts. And they are reporting hot stock tips? Interesting.

One final point. Some stock recommendations will not work out. It's impossible for these newsletters to have a 100% track record over time. So be aware of this. And know there are ways to minimize losses, which we will cover later in the book.

That said, I think good newsletters really help improve your odds of investing success. So with all that in mind, here are a couple of dividend stock newsletters that fit my requirements. And as of this writing, I subscribe to them, and have been pleased with them both.

So one or both of them may be useful for you as well.

The Oxford Income Letter

The Oxford Income Letter is a great value in my opinion, and I read it regularly.

This newsletter is part of the Oxford Club, which began publishing under that name in the mid 1980's. So these newsletters have been around for a while and have a pretty good track record. If you're interested, here's a link to the history of the club and the newsletters - http://oxfordclub.com/the-oxford-clubs-beginnings/.
The newsletter follows two of my key requirements. First, it gives specific recommendations, i.e. they will say "Buy this stock up to this price." And second, you can subscribe for a very reasonable price of about $49 a year.

Compare that cost to using a full-service broker. If you took one of his recommendations, and ask him to place the order for you, he would probably charge you around $60 in commission - for that one order. There's nothing wrong with that if you don't want to place your orders in your own online account. I'm just showing you the newsletter price for an entire year as a comparison to that one-trade cost.

Full-Service Broker Commissions: Full-service commissions can vary significantly from one firm to another. Commissions can be as low as $30 per trade or as high as $300. Some full-service firms also have brokers who use a discount commission rate to be competitive with other online brokers. And some also have a reduced broker-assisted commission rate that ranges from $30 to $40 per trade.

As the name implies, *The Oxford Income Letter* focuses on income producing investments, including dividend paying stocks and other income type funds. For example, looking at my latest *Oxford Income Letter*, they are recommending a technology stock that is currently paying a 7% dividend, and has continually increased its dividend over the past years. The stock price is very low, and there are good reasons to believe it will grow from here.

So this is one of those dividend stocks that also grows in value plus paying you a dividend. That's great - you are getting the best of both worlds here.

Their Chief Income Strategist is Marc Lichtenfeld. And, as they say, he offers cutting edge insight every month on how to create an unbeatable income portfolio. He provides picks and analysis on dividend stocks, and provides updates on three stock portfolios, which you can follow depending on your objectives. These portfolios are…

- **The Retirement Catch-Up/High Yield Portfolio** - with emphasis on current high yields.
- **The Instant Income Portfolio** - with emphasis on income for today.
- **The Compound Income Portfolio Dividend** - emphasizing reinvestment for tomorrow.

For those wanting to invest in dividend paying stocks, that should grab your interest. And those three portfolios look pretty interesting, don't they?

As of this writing, subscription was $49 for a year. And they offer a 90-day no-risk trial subscription. So if you are interested in this newsletter, you can look their site over here http://oxfordclub.com/income-letter/. And you can subscribe at that link if you like as well.

The Daily Paycheck

Not much embodies the paychecks and raises concept of dividend stocks better than *The Daily Paycheck* newsletter. As they say on their website, each monthly issue is loaded with fresh tips to help you reach the goal of receiving a fat dividend check for every day of the month.

The newsletter was started by Amy Calistri about six and a half years ago. To add a little color to the story, her signature photo always showed her wearing a cool hat. But hats aside, what she has done with her newsletter, and her portfolio, is truly remarkable.

She started out being funded with $200,000 by her employer, The Street Authority. And in those brief six and a half years since she launched the newsletter, its portfolio has generated $102,719.22 in dividends. And the portfolio is now valued at $330,327, for an overall return of 65.2%.

Amy's passion for writing about dividend stock investing has come through in every newsletter. Sadly, she recently left that job to help her Mother with a health issue. But even as she took on this new challenge, she showed her belief in the value of dividend stocks.

As she said in her final email, she considered herself fortunate on many fronts. She quoted a Federal Reserve survey stating that "46% of Americans do not have enough money to cover a $400 emergency expense."

And then went on to say, "But that's not true for me. I've been lucky enough to practice what I preach. After years of writing *The Daily Paycheck*, I have a healthy income-producing portfolio -- one that can easily see me through a period without employment."

Such is the power of dividend stock investing. And to beginning to build your future paychecks and raises starting today.

Similar to *The Oxford Income Letter*, her portfolio is made up of three major portfolios. They are…

- **High-Yield Opportunities Portfolio** - to help maximize your overall portfolio's income.
- **Fast Dividend Growers Portfolio** - to help maximize your overall portfolio's income growth.
- **Steady Income Generators Portfolio** - to help to minimize your portfolio's overall risk, while providing a dependable stream of income.

What I particularly like about her newsletter is that it calls out many monthly dividend paying stocks. These really begin to feel like monthly paychecks. And of course, the rather ambitious goal of ultimately arranging these investments in such a way that you are getting a dividend check every day. That's even better.

As of this writing, she's turned the newsletter over to Genia Turanova, the new Chief Investment Strategist. Genia is an experienced money manager who has also been writing and editing financial articles and newsletters for many years. And while she doesn't wear the cool hat like Amy did, I expect she will keep the concept of the Daily Paycheck the same.

I recently renewed my subscription for two years and look forward to reading many more issues and Genia's future recommendations.

And here's the good news. My renewal was only $79, so that's less than $40 per year. That's a very reasonable price for the true value you receive on every page. And they offer a 90-day no-risk trial subscription.

So if *The Daily Paycheck* concept and newsletter looks interesting, you can look over their site, and subscribe if you like at http://www.streetauthority.com/how-start-earning-paycheck-every-day-year-30427989.

6

WHAT YOU NEED TO GET STARTED

There's just one more thing you need to do before you can buy your first stock. And that is to open a stockbroker account.

Think of it this way. Just like you need a bank account to do your banking, you need a stockbroker account to do your stock investing.

You've probably had, and used, a bank account for years. So you're already familiar with banking accounts (checking, savings, etc.). **You keep your cash in your bank accounts.** And you make deposits, withdrawals, write checks and make transfers of that cash into and out of those accounts.

Similarly, **you keep your stocks in your stockbroker account** (and bonds, mutual funds, etc. - we'll focus on stocks to keep it simple). And you buy and sell stocks in that account. Interestingly, you also keep some cash for investments in that account, so that you can buy stocks. And when you sell a stock, the cash from that sale is put back into your broker account.

Once you have opened a stockbroker account, you can start investing in stocks. That is to say, you can start buying and selling stocks using that account.

To open a stockbroker account, you will need to choose a stockbroker. This is similar to when you opened your banking account. You had to choose a bank to open it with. So you may have looked at Bank of America, USBank, a regional or local bank, etc., and chosen one of them.

Similarly, you will need to choose a stockbroker to open an account with. I'll list a number of them for you, and even tell you which one I have used, quite satisfactorily, for years.

Choosing A Broker

When you choose a stockbroker (or broker) you will have to decide if you want a full-service broker or an online discount broker.

With a full-service broker, you pay the broker a commission to do your buying and selling for you. Typically, they may make stock recommendations as well. Your advantage with a full-service broker is that you won't have to learn how to place buy and sell orders, and you will have the assurance a professional is doing this for you. And you will have access to their advice and recommendations. Of course, brokers must eat, so they will charge you commissions for this service.

Or you can open an online discount broker account and do all your trading (buying and selling stocks) yourself. While that option is not free, as the name implies, the commissions for trading your online account run at a big discount to having a broker do the trades for you.

To give you an idea how big the discount is, a typical full-service broker might charge you $60 or more to buy or sell a stock for you. Compare that to discount brokers. I have seen commissions advertised as low as $4.50. And I pay around $10 with my online discount broker. That's a big difference.

Some people start by using a full-service broker, then move on to trading their own online account. Or you can start right off with an online account. It depends on your level of confidence.

In my opinion, using a discount broker is fine for most individuals. Consider that millions of people trade online today, so it is not terribly difficult if you apply what you learn here. And most discount online brokers give you the option of talking to one of their live brokers to help you through a transaction if you get confused. They will probably charge you extra for that transaction, but you can watch and learn, and then do it yourself next time at the online discount fee.

So the rest of this book is oriented toward you doing your own trading in an online discount broker account. But even if you choose a full-service broker to do this for you, all the information presented here is still valuable to you. That's because you will still want to understand what your full-service broker is telling you. And doing for you. And you will need to be able to tell them what you want them to do for you as well.

One final thought on brokers while you are choosing one. They should be friendly and helpful when you are opening your account with them. A good broker should also be accessible to you and return your calls. And a full-service broker should periodically keep you up to date on the status of your account, and they should take the time to explain any transactions that you don't understand. So if they aren't helpful when you are opening your account, choose another broker.

Of course, brokers are busy like the rest of us, so unless you have good reason, you shouldn't be calling them every five minutes — just call when you need to.

List Of Online Brokers

There are many good online discount brokers you can use. Here are some thoughts about them for you.

There are online discount brokers and super discount brokers. I tend to avoid the super discount guys. I had trouble with a super discount broker in my commodity options trading past, so I favor the more run of the mill, average discount brokers.

Some brokers that fit this description are …

- TDAmeritrade - www.tdameritrade.com

- Scottrade - www.scottrade.com

- E*Trade - www.etrade.com

- Fidelity Investments - www.fidelity.com

- Charles Schwab - www.schwab.com

Setting up and keeping an account with these brokers should be free, and the cost per trade (when you buy or sell a stock) should be around $10. Some will be more, some less.

For example, I recently saw a television commercial for Scottrade advertising $7 per trade. Since you probably won't be trading that frequently, a few dollars more or less is probably not a big deal. So I tend to choose these things based more on ease of use.

Another consideration is how many trades you may do per year. Your number of trades may range from none to no more than five or ten in some months (and that's kind of high, actually). Note that I said typically here. I may have made forty trades in one month during the peak of the market problems in 2008-2009 – but that is not typical.

Another consideration is whether you work in an office during the day and want to occasionally check on your stocks. In this case you may be accessing your online stockbroker account through your employer's computer. You will want to make sure the broker you chose can be accessed through your companies' computer firewall.

I can tell you from personal experience that TDAmeritrade works fine through the firewalls of companies I've worked for in the past, and I have read that Scottrade is set up this way as well.

The others listed above may very well work too, but you will want to verify this up front with them when you are setting up your stock account.

Opening An Account

To open an account, you will need some basic information such as…

- Your Social Security Number or Individual Taxpayer Identification Number (ITIN)
- Your employer name and address

It should take just a few minutes to fill out the application for a simple, individual account. And it is not complicated if you are making an initial cash deposit to set it up.

It gets a bit more involved if you are opening an IRA account, and transferring stocks and funds into it from 401k's you've had with previous employers. If you are doing this, then you will need a copy of your 401k accounts before you start. But don't be put off by this additional paperwork.

This is actually a good idea to consolidate your old 401k's into one account that you can manage. Otherwise, they are just sitting there, going up and down based on the whims of the market. And probably costing you too much in fees, as they are notorious for that. Also, you will have many more investment choices in your new consolidated account.

When I was a broker, I often helped people consolidate all of their old 401k's, which they couldn't do anything with, into a new account. This way they could take control of their future, and trade and direct these funds they had accumulated from past employers.

So if you want to start investing in stocks, take the time to open your broker account. And remember, you only have to do this once. Then you are good to go.

The Online Broker That I Use

I have used TDAmeritrade for much of my personal investing for over eleven years and been very satisfied with them. They are responsive in case I need to call them – which is rare – and I have recommended them to my friends.

To put that in context, when I was a stockbroker, I had my personal account with the national broker dealer I worked for. And as you can imagine, it had full online capabilities. But once I left the brokerage, I moved my account to TDAmeritrade, which also offered me all of the online capabilities I need.

One final thing to mention here. Outside of having my personal accounts with TDAmeritrade, I have no affiliation with them. And I receive no compensation for mentioning that I use them. I am simply relating to you my personal experience.

So feel free to choose whichever broker you like.

But don't agonize over this. Just choose one and get on with it. This is literally your last step you need to take before you can start buying and selling stocks. So if you just can't make up your mind, you can do what I did and just choose TDAmeritrade.

So get started on opening your account. Because we are getting ready to show you how to buy your first stock.

7

SMART WAYS TO BUY DIVIDEND STOCKS

At this point let's say you've picked out a great dividend stock to buy.

You've done your due diligence and checked the stock out. That is to say that you know it pays a dividend, the dividend increases, and the payout ratio indicates the company can keep paying you the dividend.

Or you've done your due diligence the easy way. You subscribed to a financial newsletter so they did all the research and due diligence for you. And their latest issue had a great story about a stock you are just itching to buy.

So now you can go out and buy your stock.

In this section you'll learn a number of smart ways to buy it. And most of them involve buying it at the best possible price. These are techniques the professionals use to do just that. Because they know the price they buy at is key to the success of their investment.

I use these professional techniques all of the time. And you can use them too.

So let's talk about smart ways to buy your dividend paying stock.

The Less You Pay The Higher Your Dividend Yield

When buying dividend stocks, here's a key point to understand. And that is that the less you pay for the stock, the higher your dividend yield percent will be. And that can make a big difference in how much it pays you over time.

Let's look at Microsoft as an example. You really like it because they have a 12% dividend increase every year. And let's say you can buy it at $35 a share. It's paying a $1.05 dividend, so your dividend percent would start off at 3%. ($1.05 dividend / $35 a share X 100 = 3%).

PERCENTS: Note that I added the X 100 to make it a percent, i.e. per cent just means "per hundred." As in there are 100 cents in a dollar. Sound familiar? Or you can use the % key on your calculator and get the same answer.

That looks like this. See year 1 (the first bar on the left) where your dividend percent is 3%. And notice that over time, with dividend increases, by year 10 you are getting a very nice 8.3%, and by year 15 a whopping 14.7%.

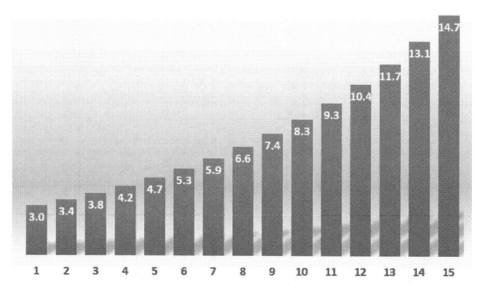

Figure 7-1. Buying Microsoft (MSFT) at 3% Yield Increasing By 12% Per Year

Now you could buy the stock at $35 a share right now. And that would be a good price. But you know that often stocks go down temporarily. This is known as a pullback. So you decide to be patient and wait a little bit. You want to see if you can buy it for $31.50 a share.

And sure enough, a few weeks later, the whole stock market corrects. And it pulls Microsoft temporarily down with it, to $31.50 a share. So you're pretty happy with that, and you buy 100 shares at that cheaper price. You strike while the iron is hot.

Now, here's the thing. Microsoft is still paying the $1.05 dividend. That didn't change just because the price went down. So because you waited and bought at the cheaper price, you are starting off with a 3.3% dividend percent to the lower price you paid ($1.05 dividend / $31.50 a share X 100 = 3.3%). And your future dividend increases look even better.

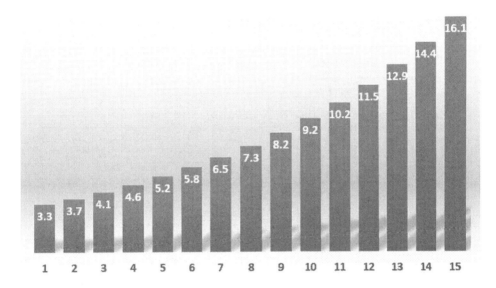

Figure 7-2. Buying Microsoft (MSFT) at 3.3% Yield Increasing By 12% Per Year

That's great. Good job. Not only did you save money with your purchase, but you are getting a higher dividend yield. That's like your friendly banker calling you and saying, "Hey, I can offer you 3.3% interest on your savings account if you want, or I can leave it at 3% - what would you like me to do?"

You would certainly choose the 3.3%. Of course, in the interest of reality, fat chance your banker will pay you 3.3%, or 3% on your savings account these days. But you get the idea - 3.3% is a much better rate than 3%.

But it gets even more interesting. Because since those dividend increases keep adding to that higher 3.3% dividend percent, they grow bigger, faster. Just look at the two charts. Now, by year 10, you are getting a great 9.2% compared to the earlier 8.3% - almost a percent higher. And by year 15 you are getting an extra-whopping 16.3%, compared to your earlier whopping 14.7% (running out of superlatives here).

So your patience will pay off. And you can see that the less you pay for your dividend stock, the higher your dividend yield percent will be. And over time, that will cause it to grow dramatically higher. Which means your dividend checks will grow dramatically higher as well.

Now that's all well and good, but you may be thinking about now, "Hey, that takes a lot of discipline to hang in there for the lower price." And you're right. But I'll show you an easy way to do this right now.

Try Not To Buy At Market

When you buy a stock, what you are really doing is placing an order. That order goes out into the stock exchanges. And some buyer, somewhere in the world, sees that order on the stock exchange, and if the price is right, they sell you the stock.

In other words, your order gets filled, usually in seconds, and you own the stock.

That's how buying a stock really happens.

Now there are two kinds of orders you can chose from.

One order is to say you want to buy the stock at whatever the price is at the moment. Or put another way, you just want to buy the shares at the **market** price. This is called a **"market order."**

Basically you are saying, "Hey, I just want to buy these shares at whatever price they cost." And typically, your order will get filled quickly at whatever price that is. And usually, the price is okay.

For example, your order might be to buy 100 shares of Microsoft stock at the market price. You can see the market price is at $35 a share when you place the order. Then, a few seconds later the order is filled. It may have been filled at $34.90, or 35.00, or 35.10. You didn't really know for sure what it would be filled at. You knew it would probably be something like $35. But with your market order, you really told the system to just buy it at any price someone would sell it to you right now.

So you can see in this example that you were at some slight risk of paying too much. Because when you say this, it's kind of like writing a blank check. And you really don't want to do that. Because in some extreme market conditions, it could come back filled at a really high price.

A better way to buy is to use another kind of order, called a **"limit order."** In this kind of order you are very specific about the highest price you will pay. Like if you said, "I want to buy 100 shares of Microsoft stock at no more than $35 a share." In other words, you **limited** the price of the order to $35 or less per share.

This is the best way to do things.

I always place limit orders. If I really want to buy the stock right now, I just look at what the current market price is, and consider that my limit. Then I place a limit order for that amount. And the order usually gets filled.

If not, and I really want to buy the stock now, I might jigger the limit price up a few cents and replace the limit order with that higher limit order. And keep doing this until it gets filled - assuming I don't have to move it up too high to where it's not a good buy.

But usually I'm not so impatient. After all, what's the hurry? Stock prices go up and stock prices go down. And I know it's really important to get a good price. So if I'm just patient and leave the order out there, I'll probably get the order filled eventually.

As a matter of fact, why not try to get the stock cheaper?

And that's the real power of limit orders. They make it easy to wait for a discounted price to come to you. Like we did in the last chapter, waiting to buy Microsoft stock at a cheaper price.

Try To Buy On A PullBack-Not The 52 Week High

So knowing that stocks go up, and stocks go down, I often try to take advantage of this and buy them cheaper. So the first thing I do is look at the stock's price history.

I go out to my stockholder account, or www.Yahoo.com/finance/, and look up the stock. And I will look for two things. They are the Days Range and the 52 Week Range.

- Day's Range - the lowest and highest price of the stock today.

- 52 Week Range - the lowest and highest price of the stock for a year.

For example, let's say Microsoft is trading at $35 a share right now. It might show the following...

- Day's Range - $33.96 - **$35.00**

- 52 Week Range - $28.43 - **$35.00**

Hmmm... so what is this telling me? It's saying that Microsoft is at the highest price it has been for the day **($35.00)**, AND the highest price it has been for the year. Now that may still be okay, and it may be worth it at that price.

And if you subscribe to a newsletter, and they recommended buying it up to $37.00 a share, then you could just go ahead and buy it at $35.00 and be done with it.

But I usually try to get it for a cheaper price. Because I know stock prices can pull back. And I like to buy them on a pullback when I can. And for me, a pullback is around 10% below the current price. So I would put in a limit order for 100 shares of Microsoft at $31.50, like our earlier example. And I might leave that limit order out there for 5 or 10 days, just to see if the stock price will come to me.

Put In A Stink Bid

You can get really crazy with this idea of putting lowball, good 'til canceled orders into the stock exchanges. Believe it or not, I have put in some orders at a 30-40% discount - AND HAD THEM FILLED!

LIMIT ORDERS: When you're placing a limit order, you specify more than just the highest price you will buy at. You also tell the exchange how long the order is good for. This is called the Good 'Til Canceled date (GTC).

For example, if today is January 1st, and you want to leave a lowball order out on the exchange for 10 days, you put January 10 in the GTC box. This costs you nothing to have this order sitting out there for the next ten days. And who knows, you might get lucky. The price might temporarily drop to your lower than market price, and you get your stock for a discount.

You'd be surprised how often this can happen. Not all of the time, of course. Maybe not even most of the time. But then, like we said earlier, what's the hurry? We want to get dividend paying stocks at the very best price. And you'll recall in our charts earlier how buying at this lower price made our dividend 3.3% as opposed to 3%.

So unless you are just in an all-fired hurry to buy this stock, try buying it at a 10% discount for a few days. After all, if your order doesn't get filled, then you can try the original price you had in mind.

And yes, sadly, sometimes the stock will have move up out of your buy range by then. So it will be too pricey to buy. But don't be too disappointed. You can do what I do. We'll just change our attitude to what I call "the Warren

SOUR GRAPES CAN BE GOOD - Or I employ my other sour grapes attitude – chuckle. I remind myself that stocks are just like busses. If you miss one, another will come around in 5 minutes. Remember that with our sources of good stock ideas, and newsletters, we will keep getting new stock recommendations coming to us to look at in case we missed out on this one.

But quite often, you will get your stock order filled at a discount. Or in the worst case, you'll be able to buy at your original price. And that is very worthwhile.

So worthwhile, in fact, that you can really push this technique to the limit if you like. Which leads us to stink bids.

Now this won't happen very often. But it happens enough that professionals will use this technique sometimes. There's even a name for these lowball orders. They're called "stink bids." That is to say, the price bid is so low you can just imagine a seller looking at it and saying, "God, these bids really stink!"

But no matter how bad they smell, sometimes they really do get filled. And that's good for you. Especially when you know this costs you nothing to try. So you really have nothing to lose here.

Now the stocks I've bought like this are typically natural resource stocks like gold or silver companies, or small oil companies. These stocks can fluctuate like crazy. And they are seldom the types of stocks you are buying for the dividend, although I do own a few dividend paying gold and silver stocks.

So the odds of these extreme bids working out for a good dividend paying stock are somewhat low. You will probably be buying them at a more normal price, or a small discount. But there's no harm in trying a lower price for a few days.

I use these low bids for another reason as well. Sometimes, if I am enthused about five or six good stocks, but can't invest in all of them, I'll put in stink bids for all of them. I've put in bids like this with an expiration date 6 - 8 months out.

This has another benefit as well. It documents the stocks I'm interested in. So when I want to see a list of those stocks, I just go to my account and look at my order status by clicking Trade à Order Status. And a list of all these stocks I have stink bids on appears on my screen.

And they just sit out there, waiting for a price miracle to happen. And occasionally it does. And I'm always surprised. Pleasantly, I might add.

And there's still another way to try to buy stocks at a discount. And people will pay you money to do it. So let's take a look at this advanced technique now.

Advanced Buy At A Discount - Selling Puts

Believe it or not, there's a way to try to buy stocks at a discount, and have people willing to pay you for the privilege. I've bought a number of my dividend stocks this way. And it still blows my mind that people will pay me money, to sell me their stocks, at a discount.

So when this happens, I get the discount, and I get the extra money they pay me as well.

What I'm talking about here is selling options - specifically, selling uncovered, or naked puts. This is an advanced technique, so most readers won't use it. But don't be discouraged if you don't understand it. Because all of the other discount buying techniques we describe in this book are great too, and you can use them.

But for those interested in learning more, I'll go into this technique in my future books *More Stock Investing For Beginners*, and also *More Stock Options For Beginners*.

On the other hand, for those of you who have traded options, I'll briefly describe how you can do this. And for those who don't understand options, you may still want to read along, just to see some future possibilities. Because this is an amazing technique — where people pay you — to buy at a discount.

So here is the technique. Again, let's use Microsoft as an example. And in this case you've decided Microsoft is a great dividend paying stock that you want to invest in.

Let's say that it was recommended in a recent issue of a financial newsletter you subscribe to. And they said to buy Microsoft (MSFT) up to $37 a share. Microsoft is currently trading at $35 a share, so it's in the recommended buy range. And it pays a 3% dividend and increases the dividend by 12% a year.

So everything is looking good and you want to buy a 100 shares of Microsoft. Now bear with me for the next three paragraphs and then I'll explain what this does.

So you go out to your stockbroker account and look up Microsoft. Hmmm… you see Microsoft has been bouncing around a bit with the price going up and down from $33 to $37 a share. Then you look up the options chain and see that you can sell a February $34 put option for a premium of $30.

By the way, it's January 1st when you are doing this, so you know that the option has seven weeks before it expires (most options expire on the 3rd Friday of their respective month - in this case it's a February option).

So you sell a February $34 strike price option for $30. The $30 is immediately deposited in your account. Now you don't own the stock yet. The earliest you might own the stock is probably in seven weeks when the option expires.

But here is what you have done by selling the put option. You have entered into a contract with the buyer of the option. And that contract essentially says that you have guaranteed the buyer that you will buy 100 shares of his stock for $34 a share if the price goes below $34 a share in the next seven weeks, and he wants to sell.

He doesn't have to sell. But he probably will if the stock goes below $34 a share. Because what you are really doing is selling him price insurance. Which makes sense, because the contract says he will pay you $30 up front for this protection. Indeed, the $30 he pays you is called a "premium." Sounds like insurance, doesn't it.

Then you wait as seven weeks goes by. And one of two things happens.

The price of Microsoft stays above $34. The option buyer keeps his 100 shares, so you don't get to buy them. But you keep the $30 premium. That's free money, just for trying to buy at a discount.

Or, the price of Microsoft is $34 or below. Let's say the stock went down to $33 a share. In this case the option buyer sells you his 100 shares for $34 a share and you keep the $30 premium.

In the first case, you made $30 but didn't get the stock. So you can try this again. Rinse and repeat, collecting about $30 every time you do it until you get the stock. ~~~

In the second case, you bought the stock for $34. That's $1 a share lower than the $35 price you were going to pay when you put this trade on anyway. So you saved $100 since option contracts are for 100 shares. That is to say, you bought the stock at a discount of $100. Plus, you kept the $30 premium. So you made $130 in the process of buying a nice dividend stock you wanted. And for a dollar a share less than you were going to pay originally. Or put another way, you bought the stock for $1.30 per share discount.

You got someone to sell you their shares, of a nice dividend stock you wanted, at a discount. And they paid you $30 for the privilege.

NOTE: Some people, myself included, sell options just to get the premium as income. And we kind of hope we don't get the stock sold to us at a discount. But we're careful to only sell options on stocks we want to buy, just in case they do get put to us.

A word of caution here – don't use this technique unless you really understand it, because you could lose money.

This technique always reminds me of the story in **Tom Sawyer** where he charged his friends money for the privilege of helping him whitewash the fence outside Aunt Polly's house. This is the closest thing to that in real life and the financial world that I know of. Nice, isn't it.

Now before we move on, don't be discouraged if you didn't follow all of that. You don't need to use this advanced technique, and in fact most people won't.

But here's another discount buying technique you can use. And it's great if you're just really itching to buy your latest dividend stock idea. And you're worried about missing out on the deal.

Break Your Purchase Into 3-4 Lower Buys

Here's another professional buying technique, and a great way to satisfy that urge you have to just buy the stock now. And still maybe get part of it at a discount.

So you have this great dividend paying stock in mind. It's paying a 3% dividend today. And even better, it has been raising its dividend by 12% a year. Wow. Fantastic. You are really jazzed about this one.

You want to buy. You are chomping at the bit to buy - right now. And it's at a good price. But in the back of your mind is that disturbing little voice that keeps saying, "Hey, why don't you try to buy it at a discount?" But you really don't want to wait.

So here's what you can do to get the best of both worlds. You can break up your purchase into three or four orders at lower and lower prices.

Let's take Microsoft as an example. You want to buy 100 shares. And it is currently at $33 a share. Which you feel is a really good price. You want to buy now. But you also think you should try for a discount. You are conflicted.

So in this example, just break your order into three parts. Put the following limit orders into your stockholder account - good for three months, let's say.

- A limit order for 33 shares at $33 a share.
- A limit order for 33 shares at $32 a share.
- A limit order for 34 shares at $30 a share.

Remember, it cost you nothing to put in these orders, although you will pay a commission on each one that gets filled.

Now here's what you just did.

Your first limit order of 33 shares at $33 will probably fill immediately. Because that's what the current price is. And that's great for your mental state. Because you were so enthused you were just dying to buy this stock. So now you've satisfied that big itch. Now you are thinking more calmly and rationally.

So with your second order of 33 shares at $32 a share, you are being a good stock investor and trying for a $1 discount. Because you remember the lower your buy price, the higher your dividend yield. And who knows, the market could easily come down $1 and get filled at the lower price. So now you feel good about yourself because you are also trying to buy at a discount. You feel like a responsible investor.

And your third order for $30?

Well, now you're getting aggressive here. You're going for a 10% discount. It may not happen. But it's not unrealistic either. Stocks certainly can drop 10% over a three-month period. And if it does, you're sitting there ready to scoop up that big discount. Now you're feeling like a professional investor. You've got your Warren Buffett attitude on.

See what you just did there? You satisfied your strong urge to buy, and you also set yourself up to buy at a discount. That's the best of both worlds.

So at this point, you can just forget about the rest of your order and see what happens over the next three months. You've just set it to forget it.

Or, if you still want to buy after a few days, what the heck, you can raise the price of the second order and just go ahead and buy. After all, as we said, you tried.

But the other nice thing about this technique is that over time, your enthusiasm has a chance to cool off a bit. And that's a good thing. Stock investing can be emotional. So your thinking may be clearer a few days out. Then you can reevaluate the last order or two, assuming they didn't fill, with a cool, rational mind. And adjust accordingly.

Turbocharge With Dividend Reinvestment

Dividend reinvestment is by far one of the best ways to buy dividend stocks. Not only is it simple, and efficient, but as we saw in Section 2, it can double or triple your wealth building over time.

Now there are two key areas of dividend reinvestment to understand. The first is just pure dividend reinvestment. And the second involves a stock purchase plan, with dividend reinvestment.

In pure dividend reinvestment, you buy a stock and then take any future dividends you receive from it and purchase more shares of the stock. So over time your original stock investment grows through compounding.

What is particularly attractive about this is that you can put all of this on automatic pilot. You can direct your stockbroker, or online stock account, to do this for you so you never have to deal with it -- once you've set it up. Your stock pays a dividend and the dividend automatically buys more shares, without you having to go out and buy them yourself.

Even better, these additional purchases are often done commission free. So over time you save a lot in reduced commissions.

And the second method, using a stock purchase plan with dividend reinvestment, works the same way. Except not only are you reinvesting dividends, but you are buying additional shares on top of that on a regular basis, thus growing your investment even faster. And again, these purchases are often commission free. And the additional purchases can be made automatically as well - typically with money withdrawn from your checking account.

This is truly set it and forget it stock investing. And it has one other great advantage that makes you an investing genius. And that has to do with you regularly purchasing a similar dollar amount of stock, month by month or quarter by quarter. Which means if the stock price is high, you buy less shares. If the stock price is low, you buy more shares.

For example, let's say you own ABC stock. It pays you a monthly dividend of $100. And you have your broker automatically withdraw another $100 monthly from your checking account to buy even more shares. So you are buying $200 of ABC stock every month. Which means if ABC stock is $50 a share, you buy four shares this month.

Now let's say ABC stock goes down to $25 a share next month (a bit extreme but go with me on this to illustrate the point). That means next month you would automatically buy eight shares. In other words, you bought twice as many shares for your $200 when the stock was low. Then the following month, ABC shares jump up to $100 a share (Wow - this stock is really volatile).

So you would only buy two shares with your monthly $200 purchase. Or put another way, you bought far fewer shares when the stock was high.

And this is what makes you an investing genius. Because you are buying the most shares when the price is low, and the least shares when the stock is high. Which plays right into the first part of the old stock market adage of "buy low, sell high."

And you didn't have to do a thing. This all happened automatically.

This concept is called dollar cost averaging, and is a very successful investing technique. And by setting up your stock purchase plan and dividend reinvestment, you are doing it effortlessly.

So this is why I said dividend reinvestment (and automatic stock purchase) is one of the best ways to buy dividend paying stocks.

If you work for a company with a 401k plan and you are investing in it, you are probably already doing this. Your employer is withholding part of your check and automatically buying more shares for you each pay period. And probably reinvesting any dividends too.

If you are using a broker outside of work, or an online broker, you can tell them to automatically reinvest your dividends for you.

And you can invest directly with many companies as well, through their DRIP (Dividend Reinvestment Programs). In this case, you will typically need to buy or own at least one share of stock to enroll. But then you can have them automatically start buying more shares with your dividends, and typically also set up an additional regular stock purchase schedule.

To learn more about these three methods of dividend reinvestment, read on.

Reinvest Through Your Employer 401K or Stock Investment Plan

If you are still working, and the company you work for has a dividend paying stock, then they may have a dividend reinvestment program set up. This may be in separate stock purchase plan, or done within your company's 401k.

This is one of the easiest ways to do dividend reinvestment. The dividends may just automatically be set to buy more shares. Or you may have to elect to do it. But either way, this is one of the best and easiest ways to reinvest those dividends. That's because once you enroll, or set it up, it all happens automatically.

And your stock position and wealth just keeps on growing.

I've participated in a couple of these in my career, and it was amazing how large the dividends could become over the years. And I'm talking five figures per year here, so it wasn't trivial.

Another advantage is that these stock purchases are often commission free. So not having to pay a commission gives you even more money that is invested in your company's stock. And some plans even buy the stock for you at a discount, like 5% or better.

So this is definitely worth checking out with your employer.

The only disadvantage is that you may be limited to purchasing just your employer's stock. So you want to make sure you don't become overinvested in just that one stock. Because that leaves you vulnerable should your employer's stock suffer a serious loss. Or worse yet, should your employer go out of business.

Remember ENRON in this case. Employees who had all of their investments tied up in the company stock got wiped out when the fraud at the company was exposed. By 2001, the stock they had in their 401k had already lost 94% in value.

So don't put all of your eggs in one basket (we discuss this even more later). That said, if this type of plan is available to you, it is worth checking out.

Another way that dividend reinvestment may be available to you in your 401k is in other funds besides your company's stock. Most 401k's offer funds you can invest in. And many of these pay dividends as well. And those dividends can typically be reinvested into buying more of the funds.

401k's are beyond the scope of this book, and vary widely, so you will need to check yours out with your employer. But it's worth looking into because they are a good way to do dividend reinvestment. And you may be pleasantly surprised with what your employer offers.

But what if your company doesn't offer these options? Or what if you want to do dividend reinvestment with other stocks?

Well, there's a way to do that too.

Reinvest Direct With Company

There are over 1100 publicly traded companies that offer their own direct dividend reinvestment programs (DRIPS).

DRIP investment programs are often offered by companies committed to dividends and long-term investors. Many of these companies have long histories of continuous dividend payments, and dividend increases. That makes this is a good area to look into for good dividend stocks to invest in.

So how do you invest in the DRIP program for a specific company that you have in mind? Well, one way is to go out to the company's web site. Most companies have a Stockholders Services section on their site. You can go there and see if they have a dividend reinvestment program.

For example, if you were interested in AT&T, then you could go out to their site at www.att.com. Then you would click on Stockholder Services. Then click on Dividend Reinvestment. And that would take you to a page on how to sign up to participate.

Note that you can try getting there directly by doing a Google search. For example, I got to the AT&T page by simply putting in the search terms "how to invest in drip program for AT&T."

Some companies administer their own program, and some have it administered by a third party. For example, AT&T's program is administered by Computershare Trust Company, N.A. So you would contact Computershare at 1 800 351-7221 for information or to enroll. Information and enrollment materials are available online at www.computershare.com/att.

Typically, you will have to own (or buy) at least one share of stock to get into the program, although I see a few that require 100 shares. Then you can set things up to have dividends automatically reinvested. Better yet, if you can afford to, set it up to purchase a certain dollar amount of shares each month through the program.

And then you are on your way. From that point on you are in set it and forget it mode. Your account will be growing its number of shares. Your dividends will be automatically reinvested. And you will be a brilliant investor because you will be dollar cost averaging, i.e. automatically buying more shares when the share price is cheap, and fewer shares when it is expensive.

Note that this would be a great gift for you or your friend's newborn child. After all, they have decades ahead of them. So you could buy a few shares for them and just let this grow. I can't think of a better gift for a new little person coming into this world, than for someone to start right off building their future paychecks and raises, can you?

8

PROTECTING YOUR DIVIDEND STOCK INVESTMENTS

We've said that dividend stock investing is close to a set it and forget method to grow your wealth. And while this is true, you will still want to check up on your stocks from time to time.

This is especially true when the stock price is going down. And not so important when the stock price is going up.

Of course, it's a great feeling when your dividend stocks are going up, because your total value is going up. But outside of feeling good, there's nothing in particular that you need to do. Because with good dividend stocks, you want to hang on to them to keep collecting bigger and bigger dividends. So you are not poised attentively, looking for some higher target price to sell at, like you might be with speculative stocks.

But when the price is going down, you will want to pay particular attention. Because you will be deciding how far the stock price can go down before the dividend isn't worth it, and you need to sell to stop your losses.

This is one of the most difficult decisions faced by investors. Because you need a way to cut your losses by knowing when to sell your stocks and exit your position.

But here's the good news. In this section we show you a very simple way to make that decision. And we show you other ways to minimize your risk, and protect your dividend stock investments as well.

This technique is different for dividend stocks, as opposed to speculative stocks. But the good news is that is the easiest technique of all.

Controlling your losses is vital to your success. Because losses, like gains, will always occur off and on with stock investments. But small losses don't matter if you control them.

So if you have a well thought out exit strategy and you execute it consistently, this can serve as a solid way to get rid of your losers before they do any real damage to your account. And similarly, identify and keep your winners as they pay you month after month, quarter after quarter.

There are only two main things you need to understand to do this. And both are simple to understand.

Don't Lose Too Much (Stop Losses)

One of the most important ways we minimize our risk occurs when our stick price is going down. Because at some point, if the stock keeps going down, we will want to "stop" our losses. This activity is actually called using "stop losses," so that's a new term for you here.

In order to set a stop loss, we actually decide up front, when we buy a stock, how much we are willing to lose before we throw in the towel and sell it.

Making this decision up front is the best time to do this. That's because you have no money on the table yet, so you are more objective. Let me say that another way. When you have bought a stock, i.e. you have money on the table, it's emotional. So the idea here is to get the emotions out of the process before buying the stock.

So we decide, up front, how much loss, what percent drop from our buying price, we will allow before we decide it's time to get rid of the stock.

And a good stop loss percent to use is 25%. This means if you invested $1000 in a dividend paying stock, and it went down by $250, so it's only worth $750, you sell it and take the $250 loss.

Why 25% you ask? Well, some credible research and back testing against the stock market has shown that stop losses in the 21% - 27% range have yielded the most efficient results as far as protecting investments.

Setting the stop losses too small, say 10%, caused people to sell their investments too early and too often, only to see them turn around and go higher. And larger stop losses, say 40% to 50%, allowed too much of a loss before bailing out of a stock in a downward trend.

Sounds simple enough, right? But let me caution you about that. Because this is one of those things that is "simple, but it ain't easy."

Here's why. Because when one of your stocks starts losing money, you will want to hang on to that stock. Back to your $1000 investment, when it goes down to $750, you will think, well, maybe it will come back up to $1000, and I won't lose any money. Every molecule in your body will be screaming to hang on to that stock, and not take the 25% loss – because you just know it will come back up.

Don't do this. Don't hang on to that stock. Because here's what can happen.

The stock may continue to go down. So now you're down by 35%. But hey, you still have hope, so you hang on. Then it's down by 50% -- now you've just got to hang on because you've lost half your money and you want to recover it.

Then it's down 75%, and you are so depressed you don't know what to do. But it keeps going down. Now you're down 90%, so you think, well, I might as well keep it, because I've lost most of my money anyway.

And sadly, you are correct. You have lost the money.

Or, as the legendary investor Warren Buffett says, there are two great rules for investing. They are ...

> **Rule 1: Don't lose the money.**
> **Rule 2: See Rule Number 1.**

You broke rule number 1, "Don't lose the money." And rule number 2 also, come to think of it. Looking back on it, you really, really, really wish you had sold that stock when it was only down 25%, right? That 25% loss doesn't look so bad now.

So don't let this happen to you. Be smart, and if your stock goes down 25%, get out while you still have 75% left. Because that will leave you with most of your money to invest in another stock, one that may go up and make you money.

So you will live to invest another day. But if you ride it all the way down to a 90% loss, you are dead in the water. You will have to start all over again.

So those are the basics of stop losses for dividend stocks. ***Sell your stock if it goes down 25% from you purchase price.*** By the way, this is also known as a hard stop loss.

A hard stop loss differs from the stop loss technique we describe for speculative stocks where you are looking to profit from stock price growth. In that case we suggest using a technique called a trailing stop loss.

With trailing stops, you sell if the price drops 25% from the highest price since you owned the stock. This is an excellent technique we cover in *More Stock Investing For Beginners*. That method helps you lose even less, and even bail out of a losing stock at a profit sometimes.

But for stocks you have bought that are paying you nice dividends, you don't care as much if the share price bounces up and down because you are still earning income. So having a hard stop can allow you more room to stay in the game, and keep those dividend checks coming in.

Warren Buffet believes in this concept so much with his dividend stocks that he says he would keep his Coca Cola stocks even if they went down by 40%. Of course, he has considerably more capital to back him up, so we won't go quite that far.

But for dividend paying stocks, we keep it simple with the 25% hard stop loss. And fortunately, this type of stop is also the easiest to use. So if you can just keep to this simple rule, you will be way ahead of most investors. ~~~

HOW TO CALCULATE YOUR STOP LOSS: Here's a shortcut you can use to calculate how low your stock can go before you need to sell it, i.e. what your stop loss amount is. Just multiply how much you paid for the stock times .75. If your stock has gone lower than that, it's time to sell.

For example, let's say you bought a stock for $100 a share. Then your stop loss amount is $75 (100 X .75). If your stock is now worth less than $75, you should sell it to keep from losing any more money. Or another example: You bought another stock for $43.95 a share. Your stop loss is $32.96 ($43.95 X .75). So if this stock is now worth less than $32.96, you should sell it.

Or, even easier, your stockbroker account will probably show what percent loss, or gain, you have with each of your stocks. In that case, if the percent loss shows higher than 25% for one of your stocks, then you should sell that stock.

Stop Loss Less Dividends

Here's an alternate way to use hard stop losses with your dividend stocks. And that is the stop loss less dividends technique.

Recall that the simple method is to sell your stock if the price goes lower than 25% of your purchase price. But if you really want to hang on to a good dividend paying stock, this method could keep you in the game a bit longer.

It works like this. Let's say you bought a stock that is $100 a share. And it pays a $3 dividend per year - or 3%. And you've owned it for two years so far.

Now the simple 25% stop loss rule would mean that if the stock goes down 25% to $75 a share, you would sell the stock to avoid any more losses. But in the stop loss less dividends, you first subtract the dividends you've received from your cost of that $100 stock.

So that would mean your true cost of buying the stock was $94 ($100 - $3 - $3). And 25% of $94 is $23.50. So subtracting that from your new cost of $94 means the stock could go down to $70.50 (as opposed to $75) before it is time to sell it.

So you can justify this as a more accurate way of calculating your stop loss.

What's the downside? Well, realize you may lose more money in a significant and continued drop in stock price. But at least you will have a rationale for your decision, as opposed to pure emotion or no plan at all. Which is what most people do.

Also, this method requires more effort to calculate your hard stop price. And most people won't go to this effort. Especially since your overall loss percent is typically shown on your stockholder account screen. After all, it's displayed right there in front of you with no effort on your part. And we all tend to follow simple rules more than complicated ones. So that recommends the 25% hard stop rule for most investors instead of the hard stop less dividends method.

I tend to do a little of both. I normally use the 25% hard stop rule. Then, if the stock drops to 25%, I go check out the dividends I've received so far and deduct them from the cost. If the stock is above that line, and I still think well of the company's future, I will hang on to it.

But if the stock has dropped even below the hard stop less dividends line, then I get rid of it. There is no rationale remaining to keep it. It has failed both stop loss tests. And if I've been thinking of selling it anyway, and I wouldn't buy it today, I will sell it even if it passes the 25% stop less dividends test.

So the choice is yours. Either method is good, because you are investing with a plan.

But if the stop less dividends is too much work for you, or confusing, just use the straight 25% stop loss rule. You will still be way ahead of most investors.

EXTRA INFO. One way to have the stop less dividends tracked for you automatically is with a service called TradeStops. This software tracks all of your stocks and automatically takes the dividends received into consideration. Then it will send you an alert if the stock drops below you adjusted stop loss line.

I've used Tradestops for years, although I typically use it for speculative stocks, not dividend stocks. As of this writing it costs around $89 per year, so it may be a little pricey for some people. But it's a great service if you really need it. You can learn about it more here at their web site www.TradeStops.com.

Don't Buy Too Much (Asset Allocation)

Now we get to the second way you protect yourself from losses. And that relates to the old saying of "don't put all of your eggs in one basket." And this is good advice, because if you drop the basket, all of your eggs are broken. Given that we are talking your future financial nest egg here, it is particularly appropriate.

So put another way, we don't want to invest all of our money in just one stock. Which makes a great deal of sense. But believe it or not, this happens more often than you may think.

One common way this happens is in employee's stock investment plans and 401k's. These are great plans to participate in. But for many employees, too often this winds up being the only stock they are invested in.

Why? Because it is so easy to do. They signed up for a plan to automatically buy company stock through a payroll deduction. And they may get this stock at a discount, making things even more tempting. Then maybe their employer matches some of their contribution, and pays it by adding even more company stock to their account each year. Furthermore, let's say the company stock is doing really well, so they want to keep concentrating on adding more of this stock.

So over the years, they accumulate a big nest egg of that stock. But that is all they have. Just one stock.

That's way too much risk. Because what if something bad happens to the company and it gets in financial trouble. If this happens, their one stock investment goes down, maybe radically. Worse yet, their company's financial condition may get so bad that they wind up laid off. So now they have lost their income from their job, and a big part of their stock account.

That's not a happy story. And it can happen.

Like ENRON, for example. There were people that had their entire retirement investment in this one company's stock. Then one day they woke up and there was that bad headline in the news. It said that the management had been cooking the books and reporting profits that were completely made up.

The stock value dropped, plummeted actually, and lost half of its value in just one week. And by the end of the scandal, and bankruptcy, the stock had dropped from $90.00 to $.61 a share. That's right, sixty-one cents. It was a total wipeout.

So whenever you are tempted to put all your eggs in one basket, you might take a minute to read about the Enron scandal. It's a sobering and cautionary tale for all investors. You can read about it here at https://en.wikipedia.org/wiki/Enron_scandal.

A better way to do this is to research the other investments your company plan offers. Now many of these plans offer very limited choices. And the choices are typically funds, like growth funds, income funds, growth and income funds, bond funds, international stock funds, etc. I actually worked for a large corporation for years that offered only three choices. They were a government bond fund, the S&P 500 fund, and company stock. But this still offered a form of diversification.

Interestingly enough, back then I was one of those employees that concentrated on just the company stock. Because it seemed to go up 15% a year. And it paid a good dividend.

I was lucky I didn't get creamed with that type of concentration. So I got away with it. But looking back, I would have done better putting part of my investment in government bonds and the S&P 500 as well.

So if possible, you want to spread your investments around in these plans, and don't get too concentrated in just one investment.

The other way investors get too concentrated comes down to greed. Let's say you have a $100,000 portfolio. And you find a stock that pays a 12% dividend. These actually exist, by the way.

So you're thinking, hey, I can invest my entire $100,000 in that one stock, and I will get $12,000 a year in dividends. Which is $1000 a month. That's a nice extra paycheck coming in every month.

But don't do it. Because if something happens to that one stock you are concentrated in, you have big problems. You will probably lose a significant portion of your original investment. And the company may need to cut the dividend, or worse yet, eliminate it just to try to survive.

Better to spread it around to other dividend paying stocks. And I wouldn't concentrate on finding too many more 12% dividend paying stocks. Because many of them are a bit iffy as far as continuing to pay that dividend.

So what is the best allocation of your stock investments? Well, I would limit my investment in any one stock to 4% of my total portfolio. In other words, with a $100,000 stock account, you would not allocate more than $4000 to any one stock. This is also known as asset allocation - as the phrase above implies.

So that means if you were fully invested, you would have twenty-five different stocks. Or put another way, you would have paychecks coming in from twenty-five different companies.

Note that by using our stop loss technique in the last chapters, you actually limit your potential loss to 1%. Because you get out if any one stock drops by 25%. Since you allocated 4% to a specific stock, and 25% of 4% is 1%, you only lost 1% of your portfolio if one of your stocks went bad and you sold using the stop loss rule.

Or put another way, with the $100,000 portfolio, you allocated $4000 to a stock. The stock dropped 25%, or $1000, so you sold it. And that $1000 loss is just 1% of your total $100,000 portfolio.

Now there's a lot of safety in that. Because the chances are, something bad is not going to happen to all of your stocks. If one goes south, you still have the other 24 which may be in good shape and paying you dividends.

And that bodes much better for your financial future.

So no matter what your particular situation is, if possible, try to find ways not to concentrate all of your investment in just one area. There is more safety in diversifying and allocation your investments across many companies and funds.

And speaking of diversifying, we want to do that another way as well.

Don't Buy All Of The Same Kind (Diversification)

Just like we don't want to invest our entire portfolio into one stock, we also don't want to invest all of our different stocks in the same kind of business or industry.

For example, it would not be smart to invest in J. C. Penney's, Macys and Target. Sure, you are invested in more than one stock, but they are all retail department stores.

So what happens to your account when there is a recession and consumers stop shopping? All of your retail department stores stocks go down — all at once.

Which means your entire portfolio goes down all at once.

So you want to invest in different types of stocks. Some could be in the retail sector, some in the energy sector, and some in the communications sector, etc. This way, if one sector you are investing in is going down, there may be other sectors you are investing in that are going up. So your entire portfolio is kind of balanced and protected. And in total it doesn't bounce all over the place. So you can sleep better at night. and not panic and make some irrational changes.

This type of investing discipline is called "diversification." You diversify your stock holdings. This is what the professionals do, and you can too. By the way, this is a smart practice for speculative stocks as well as dividend stocks. Indeed, it is a smart practice for all of your investments.

Here's an overall list of the business sectors you could be invested in…

- Health Care
- Real Estate
- Energy
- Information Technology
- Consumer Discretionary
- Consumer Staples
- Utilities - Like American Electric Power Company (AEP)
- Materials
- Financials
- Industrials
- Telecommunications - Like AT&T (T).

You can see an even bigger list of these sectors, and subsectors within them at https://www.fidelity.com/sector-investing/.

So as you are buying dividend stocks, and building your portfolio, buy some in different sectors like the pros do. This one simple technique will put you ahead of most of the investors out there.

EXTRA CREDIT: Jim Cramer's Mad Money show is a great show to watch. And he has an "Am I Diversified" segment where viewers call in and tell him their top five stocks they are invested in. Then, right before your eyes, he classifies them by sector and tells them if they are well enough diversified or not. It's interesting to watch, and will get you into the diversification mindset. And it's very entertaining as well.

And it's the sign of a good stock investor. And a good way to protect your investments. Which will improve the reliability of your future paychecks and raises. And that's a good thing. Because when it comes to paychecks, reliability is key.

Checking In From Time To Time

Another way to protect your investments is to check up on them from time to time. I typically check up on my stocks a few times a day, and occasionally skip a day here and there. That's what works for me. But then, I'm kind of a stock geek. So that may be way too frequent for you.

Maybe you prefer to check up on your stocks every day or so, or a couple of times a week. I even know of a Palm Beach multimillionaire who only checks his portfolio once a week. And you can probably go longer than that by setting up automatic messages in your account to warn you if a stock value is dropping too much. So that's a pretty wide range you can fit in.

The one exception to this is when the overall stock market is dropping over a period of days. Or you have a stock that has almost lost 25% in value, i.e. it's about to hit its stop loss limit. Now you are on alert. You need to be ready to sell and cut your losses if necessary.

In this case, at a minimum, you should check up on that stock at the end of every day after the market has closed. Then, if you see the closing price of your stock has dropped below your 25% stop loss limit, you should plan to sell it the next day.

So just log in to your stock account from time to time. It's constantly updated and will show you a list of all your stocks (your portfolio) and what they are worth at that point in time.

FUN BUT NOT NECESSARY: Sometimes after I've checked on my stocks, I wait a minute and hit the refresh key again. This will show how their value has changed in that short period of time, as buyers and sellers from all around the world bought and sold in the last 60 seconds. It's kind of fun, and interesting, as you watch the world of finance in action, real time. But this is certainly not necessary, and you probably have better things to do with your time.

Come to think of it, so do I.

Another place I go to look up stocks is on Yahoo. I even used Yahoo sometimes when I was a stockbroker, if I was looking up a security we didn't have listed. To look up a stock on Yahoo, just go to www.Yahoo.com. Click the Finance section on the left of the screen. Then enter the stock symbol at the top and hit the return key.

Your stock and its current price will appear. Additionally, you can see a chart of how it has been doing over the past days, weeks, years, etc., by clicking on various time frames.

I also go to Yahoo to look at some of the comments other owners have made on the message board. You can see these by clicking the message board link on the left. Many of the comments are quite interesting. Some are informative, and others rather trivial.

All that said, you usually don't need to check on your stocks all that frequently. And as mentioned, many stock account sites allow you to set up email alerts that will trigger if a stock is dropping below your stop loss limit. This can be very handy and useful.

Are They Still Paying A Dividend?

When you are checking up on one of your stocks, an important thing to verify is if they are still paying a dividend. Because this is why you are invested in the company. These are your future paychecks we're talking about here.

Using your stockholder account, you can just look at the list of stocks you own. Then click the symbol of the stock you are interested in. A general information page will come up. And that page will show you the current annual dividend amount and the yield percent.

For example, as I was writing this, I decided to check up on Sysco, one of my favorite dividend holdings. So I clicked on SYY (its symbol) that is listed in my portfolio. And my account brought up a page that confirmed that yes, Sysco is still paying a dividend. At today's price of $48.32, it is paying $1.24 per share per year, and that is a yield percent of 2.57% for people investing today.

I also note, happily, that since I bought it back when it was $28.05 a share, my yield percent has grown to 4.4% ($1.24 / $28.05 X 100). And as you continue investing in dividend growing stocks, you will have this type of happy result as well over time.

So that's the easy way to check if you use your stockholder account.

Here's another way to do this. Your stockholder account may allow you to create different views of your portfolio. If so, you can pick the fields you want to see in that list of your stocks. For example, I created the JohnDivView in one of my TDAmeritrade accounts. I set it up to list the symbol, purchase price, dividend amount and dividend yield percent. So by just looking at my portfolio in this view, I can see, line by line, stock by stock, that they are paying dividends.

So that is much faster than looking each stock up one by one. Of course, you have to create the special view first. But that's a one-time thing, and you can save it and use it any time after that. And creating it is pretty easy. You just drag and drop the fields you want to see from a big list of fields available.

Even better, I can export this to a spreadsheet. And since I have the purchase price and the dividend amount in that view, it's a simple calculation to see what yield percent I have on each stock. Since most of my stocks have had dividend increases since I bought them, my yield percents on some of them are quite nice. And this can happen for you too.

If you don't have a stockholder account available, you can go out to www.Yahoo.com and enter the symbol in the lookup box on the screen. Then click the Search button, and a general information page will display the annual dividend amount and the yield % at the current price.

So that's how you do it. And I would encourage you to do this from time to time, maybe monthly, or quarterly. Just consider this as an overall health check on your different stocks.

And while you're at it, you might check up on this too.

Has The Dividend Continued To Go Up?

Another important thing to check is if the dividend continues to increase over time. This is important because these are your raises.

One way you can do this is in your stockholder account. It should have a section called History and Statements, or something to that effect, that you can go to. If it does, you can put in a date range of transactions you would like to see. Then you select dividends as the transaction type and select the stock (or stocks) you want to see.

This will produce a list of all the dividends you have received for the stock(s) in that date range. If you see that year by year your dividend payment into your account has been going up, you're good. Your stock is increasing its dividends. You are getting raises.

Another way to check this, without using a stockholder account, is to go to the website http://www.dividendchannel.com/ and enter the stock symbol. This will list the dividend payments for the past five to ten years for that stock (some stocks even longer). Then just review the list to see if the dividend payments have been going up year by year.

So that's a couple of ways to check your dividend growth. Be sure and do this, because these are your raises. And that's pretty important for your future paychecks, wouldn't you say.

Is There Any Unsettling News About The Company?

The last thing we check for is any special news about the company. Because news can give us a clue about the health of the company. And that's important to us getting our dividends and increases.

Fortunately, there is a wealth of news published about companies listed on the stock exchanges. And you can find it by looking in your stock account or Yahoo Finance.

For example, if you look up the symbol for one of your dividend paying stocks, you will probably see a section called something like Latest News. So, looking up Apple (AAPL) in my stockholders account as I write this, I see many recent articles like…

- Apple iMessage will bring millions to Mobile Marketing
- Apple Historic Surge Could Confirm What Buffett Already Knew
- Apple Is Failing To Bully Hollywood Into Its Future of TV
- Apple Posts Narrower Than Expected Loss

These all look pretty interesting and are the kind of articles you might click and read. They are typically pretty short, so you can look through a few of them pretty quickly.

What you are looking for is something that reaffirms the company is doing well. Or, more important, it may reaffirm something else. The company could be having problems

Now, all companies face problems from time to time. And if you own their stock, you want to know about them. Because some problems can put your dividends and dividend increases in jeopardy.

Don't Overreact

As we mentioned, all companies run into problems from time to time. So what do you do if one of your stock's companies is having problems?

Well, the first thing is to not panic. Because more often than not, the company will find ways to overcome those problems. After all, the company's CEO is working daily to keep the company profitable. His or her big annual raise and bonuses depend on it. Which means they're motivated.

So just try to understand the problem and see if it is something that can be overcome. For example, maybe their current products sales have slowed down, BUT they have a killer product just about to launch. Or maybe they had a natural disaster that slowed down one of their plants, so they have to take a one-time charge against their earnings to account for that. BUT the plant will be back in full operation next quarter.

In the long run, problems like that are probably no big deal. Indeed, they may present a buying opportunity for you to buy more stock at a lower price. Because other investors may have overreacted and done some panic selling. Which lowered the stock price. Which means you can double down if you think the company will recover.

So look through the articles and try to understand if this is a recoverable one-time thing or not. And then decide if you will keep the stock in an even-handed, rational way. Or even buy more.

The one type of news I look really hard at is if there are any accounting irregularities reported, or mention of fraud. I switch into a pretty unforgiving mood at that point. After all, if you can't count on the honesty of the management, and the accuracy of their accounting, they are probably not going to be a very solid dividend producer. So if you see too much of this kind of information, it's time to pull the plug and sell the stock.

Just get out and use this as an opportunity to start looking for a replacement stock.

Because there are plenty of other company's stocks out there run by hard-working, honest CEO's that will keep your dividends coming to you. And keep growing the company so your dividends keep growing too.

9

CONCLUSION

Now you've gained a lot of valuable information at this point. And remember, this is not just theory. You can go out and invest in a dividend stock, and have a dividend check in your mailbox within 30 to 90 days.

To recap, you've learned:

- How to create your future paychecks through dividend stock investing.
- How dividend increases become your future raises.
- How your yields can grow to 5%, 10% and even larger over time.
- How dividend reinvesting makes you a brilliant investor and compounds your wealth.
- How dividend investing is easy – and nearly set it and forget it.
- How to protect your stock investments, and a simple rule to stop your losses.
- Great sources of winning dividend stock ideas to invest in.
- And how to open a stock investment account and get started now.

It's up to you to use this information to start building your future paychecks and raises.

So I want you to immediately apply what you've learned. Don't just close this book and move on to something else. Instead, if you don't have a stockholder account, gather your information, call a broker and open your account.

Then, using newsletters and other sources of good dividend stock recommendations, make a commitment to find your first great stock to invest in. Shoot for one that pays around a 3% dividend, and increases the dividend by about 10%. Then go out to your account and buy it.

Now you are on your way. And your first paycheck will show up in your mailbox in less than 90 days. Better yet, just have the dividends reinvested if you can. Then keep finding more dividend stocks to invest in, and buy as your funds allow. Rinse and repeat.

And over time, your dividend checks and wealth will begin to grow, faster and faster, as time goes by.

And don't waste time and regret thinking you should have done this a long time ago. Yes, we all should have started dividend stock investing at an early age. But as the old adage says, "The best time to plant a tree is 20 years ago; the second-best time is now."

There's no time like the present to build your future. And now you know how to do it.

And finally, be sure and check out the my *Live, Learn and Prosper* website at http://www.LiveLearnAndProsper.com. You'll find many helpful articles on dividend stock investing, and thoughts on good dividend paying stocks.
I wish you the best of success, and many paychecks and raises in your future.

John

Would You Like To Know More

You've learned how to create your future paychecks through dividend stock investing at this point. Historically these have proven to be some of the best investments. And much of your portfolio can be invested in these lucrative, income generating stocks.

But there's another important, exciting part of your portfolio that deserves attention too. And that is investments in precious metals like gold and silver. Experts recommend that a small portion of your portfolio be invested here, typically somewhere between 5-10%.

And the best bet for the money is silver. This beautiful metal has served mankind as money, and a solid store of value, for thousands of years. Did you know that the price of gasoline has not gone up over 50 years - in terms of silver! That's right. In the late 60's, a quarter (which had 90% silver in it back then) would buy a gallon of gasoline. Today, that same silver quarter will still by a gallon of gasoline, because the silver content is worth about $3.

In my future book entitled, ***Silver Investing For Beginners***, I give the exact techniques and blueprint for...

- How you can start investing for as little as $3.
- How silver investing can lead to big profits.
- How silver preserves value and can protect your portfolio.
- And many more tricks and tips to increase your wealth.

If you want to take your investment success to the next level, then this book is for you. Click here for Silver Investing For Beginners.

Additional Resources

At this point, you've learned all the basics you need to start investing in dividend paying stocks.

I've given you the exact steps to use to get started. Essentially, these are the same steps I have come to use over the years. I say "essentially," because my path was not so simple and direct. And that is because I didn't have a book like this to get started.

But you now have the same basic system I would use to get started today.

With that said, we covered a lot of resources in the book. So this section lists them all for you as a handy reference. And there are some additional resources listed as well.

Live, Learn And Prosper
www.LiveLearnAndProsper.com

Our parent website. Many helpful articles on dividend stock investing, and thoughts on good dividend paying stocks. You can also sign up for the free monthly newsletter here at www.LiveLearnAndProsper.com/n.

Stocks That Have Increased Their Dividends For 25 Years Or More - Dividend Aristocrats
https://en.wikipedia.org/wiki/S%26P_500_Dividend_Aristocrats

Known as the Dividend Aristocrats, this is a list of S&P 500 companies that have increased **dividends** every year for the last 25 consecutive years. This can be a good place to start looking for good dividend paying stocks.

Stocks That Pay MONTHLY Dividends
http://www.dividend.com/dividend-stocks/monthly-dividend-stocks.php.

Here's a list of over 700 stocks that pay monthly dividends. Monthly dividends really start feeling like paychecks.

Dividend History
http://www.dividendchannel.com/

Shows the history of dividend payments that have been made for a stock. The history can go back ten years and more. Like most sites, just enter the stock symbol at the top and click search. This is an excellent site and I use it frequently.

Dividend Growth Rate List
http://dripinvesting.org.

The best list I have found for pre-calculated dividend growth rates. It's a little tricky to use but worth it. After going to the site at http://dripinvesting.org, click in the Info/Tools/Forms section, which will take you to the Drip Investing Resource Center page. Then click on the http://www.tessellation.com/david_fish/ link and download the most recent spreadsheet. This spreadsheet will have pre-calculated the dividend growth rates of more than 750 dividend paying stocks - all shown in one list under the CCC tab (which stands for Champions, Contenders and Challengers).

Free Stock Information and Charts
https://finance.yahoo.com/

Very useful to research a specific stock. Just enter the stock symbol at the top of the screen and click the Search Finance button. You will find a wealth of information, including the dividend amount and yield. The site also has good charts of the historical stock prices. You can also get to this site by going to www.Yahoo.com and then clicking the Finance tab.

The Oxford Income Letter

http://oxfordclub.com/income-letter/

Excellent paid subscription newsletter with monthly dividend stock recommendations.

Their Chief Income Strategist is Marc Lichtenfeld, and, as they say, he offers cutting edge insight every month on how to create an unbeatable income portfolio. He has three portfolios which are...

- **The Retirement Catch-Up/High Yield Portfolio** - with emphasis on current high yields.
- **The Instant Income Portfolio** - with emphasis on income for today.
- **The Compound Income Portfolio Dividend** - emphasizing reinvestment for tomorrow.

As of this writing, I subscribe to this newsletter and the subscription was $49 for a year. And they offer a 90-day no-risk trial subscription.

The Daily Paycheck

http://www.streetauthority.com/how-start-earning-paycheck-every-day-year-30427989

Excellent paid subscription newsletter that truly embodies the paychecks and raises concept of dividend stocks. As they say, each monthly issue is loaded with fresh tips to help you reach the goal of receiving a fat dividend check for every day of the month. Started by Amy Calistri and now run by Genia Turanova, the new Chief Investment Strategist, it has three portfolios. They are...

- **High-Yield Opportunities Portfolio** - to help maximize your overall portfolio's income.
- **Fast Dividend Growers Portfolio** - to help maximize your overall portfolio's income growth.
- **Steady Income Generators Portfolio** - to help to minimize your portfolio's overall risk, while providing a dependable stream of income.

As of this writing, I subscribe to this newsletter and the subscription was $79 for two years, so less than $40 per year. And they offer a 90-day no-risk trial subscription.

Tracking Your Stop Losses
https://tradestops.com/

Very useful if you have many different stock positions and want to use sophisticated stop loss tracking. I subscribe to it, but it is a paid for subscription service. And it's not necessary for beginners with just a few stock positions. You can use your discount brokers free alert system instead.

List Of Different Business Sectors
https://www.fidelity.com/sector-investing/.

Great list of the various business sectors, and subsectors, you can invest in. This is a good reference to help you keep your portfolio diversified.

How NOT To Invest - The ENRON Story
https://en.wikipedia.org/wiki/Enron.

Read this cautionary story about the total failure of ENRON whenever you are tempted to buy too much of one stock.

How To Find The Payout Ratio
http://www.dividend.com/dividend-stocks/.

Use this site to verify the company is making enough money to keep paying you dividends. This is known as the payout ratio. So how do you find out the payout ratio? Here's an easy way for you. Just go to the website. Then enter the stock symbol in the search box at the top and click. The payout ratio will display for you. Anything that is .70 or less is considered good.

DRIP Investing (Dividend Reinvestment Programs)

www.computershare.com/

Use this site to start dividend reinvesting. Some companies administer their own program, and some have it administered by a third party. For example,

AT&T's program is administered by Computershare Trust Company, N.A., and their information and enrollment materials are available online at www.computershare.com/att. Or you can contact Computershare at 1 800 351-7221 for information on how to enroll.

Note: You can also reinvest through your online broker - see list of online brokers. Or through many company's websites in the investor relations tab.

Dividend Aristocrats ETF (NOBL)

https://finance.yahoo.com/quote/NOBL?p=NOBL

An Exchange Traded Fund that you can invest in that tracks the Dividend Aristocrats index. This allows you to make one investment in all of the stocks that have raised their dividends for 25 consecutive years. That's pretty impressive performance!

5 Year Average Dividend Yield

https://finance.yahoo.com/quote/INTC/key-statistics?p=INTC

To find out the five-year average dividend yield. Just search on symbol you are interested in, then click the Statistics Tab. Scroll down to Dividends and Splits section.

List Of Stock Symbols

https://en.wikipedia.org/wiki/List_of_S%26P_500_companies

A handy list of the stock symbols for the top 500 companies in the United States, known as the S&P 500. S&P stands for Standard & Poor's, an organization that has been providing financial market information for more than 150 years.

Free Stock Recommendations - Jim Cramer

http://www.cramers-mad-money.com/

A web site that publishes Jim Cramer's stock recommendations from his nightly television show on CNBC called Mad Money. Not all recommendations are dividend paying stocks, so you have to be selective.

Free Stock Recommendations - Melissa Lee
http://www.cnbc.com/id/17390482.

A web site that publishes stock recommendations from Melissa Lee's Fast Money on CNBC. Not all recommendations are dividend paying stocks, so you need to be selective. Look for Final Trade articles for recommendations. Alternatively, just Google "Fast Money Final Trade" to see their latest recommendations.

Discount Broker Web Sites
1. TDAmeritrade - www.tdameritrade.com

2. Scottrade - www.scottrade.com

3. E*Trade - www.etrade.com

4. Fidelity Investments - www.fidelity.com

5. Charles Schwab - www.schwab.com

I've used TDAmeritrade for years.

More Books By John

Stock Investing For Beginners - How To Buy Your First Stock And Grow Your Money

The upper ten percent use stocks to grow their income and wealth. Here's just what you need to get started and join the club. You will be able to buy your first stock by the end of this book. Available in eBook and print format.

Stock Market For Beginners - Simple Steps To Get Started And Achieve Your Goals

If you liked *Stock Investing For Beginners*, this is a large, easy to read paperback with additional chapters covering many more useful topics. Similar to *Stock Investing For Beginners*, it covers how most wealthy people are business owners. And it reveals how stocks are the easiest way for you to become a business owner and increase your wealth. By the end of the book you will be able to buy your first stock.

Your Future Paychecks And Raises - Get Dividend Checks In Your Mailbox Paid To The Order Of YOU!

Investing in dividend stocks is one of the most profitable ways to invest. That's because YOU GET PAID while you invest. They will actually send you checks in the mail. And you don't have to wait a long time, either. You can get your first check in 30 - 90 days. Learn how to get these checks, and how they allow you to build your future paychecks and raises too. You will learn where to find these profitable stocks, how to invest in them, and start getting your first checks – PAID TO THE ORDER OF YOU. Available in eBook and print format.

Future Books and FREE First Chapters

Be sure and check out these future books by John. You can also get the first chapters for free as they become available.

Silver Investing For Beginners - Invest In REAL Money Today For A Wealthier Future Tomorrow

The dollar has lost over 40% of its value in the last ten years. But silver has served as honest money for mankind for thousands of years. Learn how investing in silver today can increase your future wealth while the dollar continues to drop. And you can invest for just $3 to begin. Even a child can use the $3 technique - and some do. Soon to be available in eBook and print format.

Stock Options for Beginners - Invest Less Money And Make Bigger Profits With Options

It's possible to make 50%, 100% and more in a few weeks or months with stock options, while investing and risking less money. Learn how to add this valuable investing technique to your skill set. Soon to be available in eBook and print format.

More Stock Investing For Beginners - Pro Techniques To Turbocharge Your Wealth

The professionals have a number of tricks they use to increase their stock investing odds for profits. You can learn them here and use them too.

More Stock Options For Beginners - Winning Strategies Of The Pros

The professionals use many different strategies to win with stock options. Imagine being able to make an investment and profit from it, even if it goes up, down, or stays the same. Learn how the pros put the odds in their favor like this.

Make More Money With Special Stock-Like Investments

There are many other types of stock-based and partnership investments you can profit from. And they are as easy to invest in as stocks. For example, there are certain special stock-like investments where you must be paid 90% of the profits by law, and the company pays no taxes on the profits. And many more to boost your investment profits.

Thank You

Before you go I'd like to say "thank you" for purchasing my eBook. I know you could have picked from hundreds of books on Kindle publishing. But you took a chance with my book.

So a big thank you for downloading it and reading it all the way to the end.

If you liked this book, then I could use your help. Could you please take a moment to leave a review of this book on Amazon.

Your important opinion and feedback will help me continue to write the type of Kindle books that help you get results. And if you really liked it, please let me know at JohnRoberts@LiveLearnAndProsper.com.

ABOUT THE AUTHOR

JOHN ROBERTS is the Founder and CEO of Live Learn And Prosper.com, a newsletter and website focused on getting the most out of investments and life. His books and articles are known for their easy to understand writing style explaining complex things.

He's been a life-long investor and was a former licensed Stockbroker, Financial Consultant and Senior Business Analyst. Prior to that, he managed the Corporate IT Department of a Fortune 100 Corporation. And yet earlier, served as the Senior Programmer/Designer for May Department Stores International, spending time in London, England designing and programming a large scale international foreign buying system. He also served in the United States Marine Corps.

But all is not work and investments in John's life. Called a renaissance man by his friends, he is also an award winning photographer, cartoonist, published author and avid sailor, believing that life should be an adventure.

He recalls one Thanksgiving finding himself singlehandedly sailing his boat the *Saline Solution* in the Florida Keys — on the far edge of tropical storm Keith. He says when he finally made it back safely to port, it was the most thankful Thanksgiving of his life. He also allows this may have been a bit too much adventure.

John's had a life-long commitment to self-improvement and achieving goals. He had an early start with higher goals as a "lettered" fiberglass pole-vaulter in high school, clearing 12' when the world record was 17'.

John currently resides in Orlando, Florida. When he's not busy writing you can often find him sailing or soaking up sun at the beach.

Made in the USA
San Bernardino, CA
20 April 2018